STORYBOOK STYLE

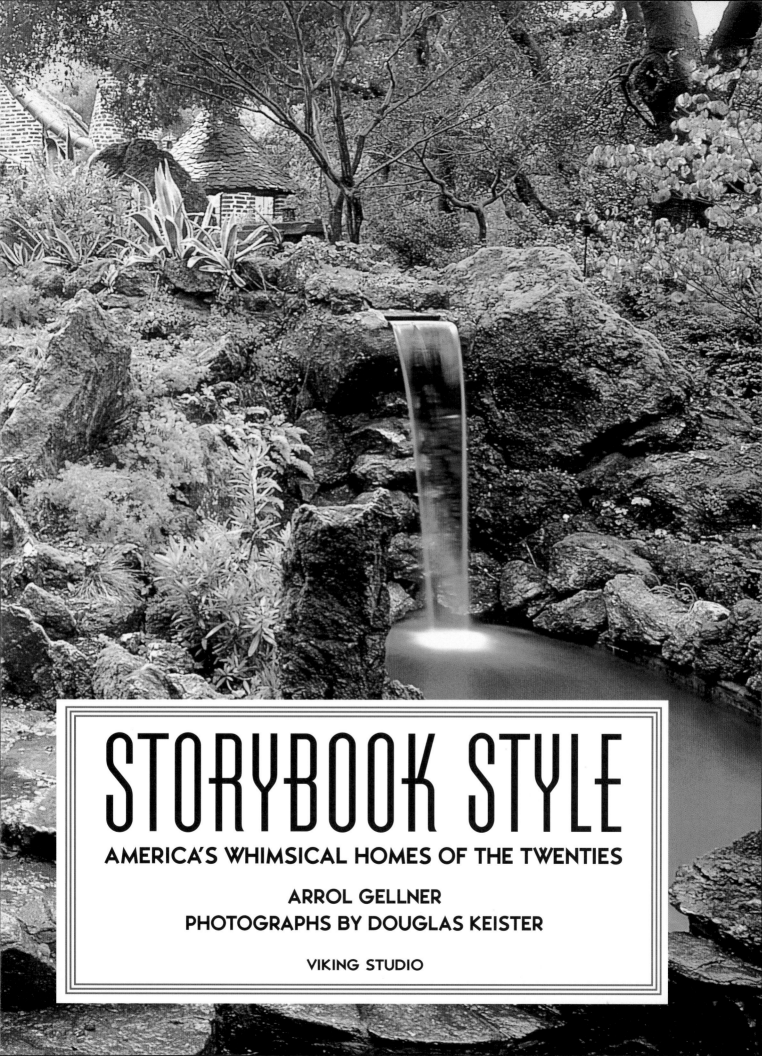

STORYBOOK STYLE

AMERICA'S WHIMSICAL HOMES OF THE TWENTIES

ARROL GELLNER
PHOTOGRAPHS BY DOUGLAS KEISTER

VIKING STUDIO

VIKING STUDIO
Published by the Penguin Group
Penguin Putnam Inc., 375 Hudson Street,
New York, New York 10014, U.S.A.

Penguin Books Ltd, 27 Wrights Lane,
London W8 5TZ, England

Penguin Books Australia Ltd, Ringwood,
Victoria, Australia

Penguin Books Canada Ltd, 10 Alcorn Avenue,
Toronto, Ontario, Canada M4V 3B2

Penguin Books (N.Z.) Ltd, 182-90 Wairau Road,
Auckland 10, New Zealand

Penguin Books Ltd, Registered Offices:
Harmondsworth, Middlesex, England

First published in the United States by Viking Studio,
a member of Penguin Putnam Inc.

First Printing, October 2001

10 9 8 7 6 5 4

Copyright © Arrol Gellner and Douglas Keister 2001
All rights reserved.

CIP data available

Book designed by Joseph Rutt
Printed and bound by Dai Nippon Printing Co., Hong Kong, Ltd.

ISBN: 0-670-89385-4

Arrol dedicates this book to his family,
for lighting the way,
and to Kathy,
for joining him on the journey.

Doug dedicates this book to Sandy,
for her love and support,
and to Mom,
for her gift of whimsy.

ACKNOWLEDGMENTS

The authors wish to acknowledge the generous assistance of the following: Bill and Marilyn Abrams; Michelle Aldridge; Bob and Annie Beaumont; Raymond Behneman; Gladys Bierman; Jean Bleuzen; Robin and Amy Bollinger; Ted Bosley; Sherri Braack; Anthony Bruce, Lesley Emmington, and Sarah Wikander, Berkeley Architectural Heritage Association; D. Burger and R. Silverman; Julie Castiglia; Gail Chick and Richard W. Frank, Lawry's Restaurants, Inc.; Hiram C. Y. and Culpernica Clegg; Brian Coleman; Joseph Dea; Paul Duchscherer; Sue Edmonds; Norm Fisher; Leslie Fitzgibbons; Julius Gaines, Picardy Drive Neighborhood Association; Jerry Gaxiola; Gloucester Publishers; Albert and Eriko Hermans; Keith and Denise Hice; C. J. Hill; William and Nancy Knudsen; Paul Lanouette; Mimi Levine; Suzy Locke; Beverly Lombardi; Sandy McLean; Sal Mendoza; Doug and Jennifer Mirner; Richey and Karen Morgan; Al and Vikkie Naccarato; Cyril I. Nelson, Penguin Putnam Inc.; Judy Pallutch; Los Payasos; Marsha Perloff; Debra Richards; Peter Roelofs; Gail Rubenstein; Enid Sales, Carmel Preservation Foundation; Sheree Sampson, Pasadena Heritage; John Sanderson; Robert Scharlach; Bob Scherer; Joel Schiller and Albert Heinzelman; Brian Schweitzer; Laura Schweitzer; Pat Smith; Larry and Beverly Stone; Bill Sturm, Oakland History Room; Elder Vides; John and Rayna Vonk; Steve Whittaker; Armand Wobo; and last but certainly not least, Linda Yeomans, Historic Preservation Planning.

CONTENTS

PROLOGUE

Fairy Tale, Disneyesque, Hansel and Gretel—these are all common synonyms for the Storybook Style, a rambunctious evocation of medieval Europe, and surely the most delightful home style of the twentieth century. Its tenure was brief: it appeared on the American scene in the early 1920s, reached its flowering shortly before the Great Depression, and was all but forgotten by the late 1930s. Storybook Style houses were the product of architects and builders with a distinct flair for theater, a love of fine craftsmanship, and not least a good sense of humor—attributes that make them especially endearing to the jaded modern eye.

Storybook Style homes are also relatively rare. They are vastly outnumbered by the ubiquitous California Bungalow, the most popular home style of the 1920s. They are uncommon even among their more straitlaced Period Revival contemporaries—Mediterranean, Normandy, and the so-called Stockbroker's Tudor—of which they are strictly speaking a subset. But while Storybook Style homes often share traits with these more upright cousins, attempting to classify them as such based upon this detail or that misses their real essence, which owes more to inventiveness than authenticity.

Three attributes set classic Storybook Style homes apart from other Period Revival styles of the '20s: their exaggeratedly plastic and often cartoonish interpretation of medieval forms; their use of artificial means to suggest great age; and last, that all but indefinable quality known as "whimsy." These are houses that embody the utmost joy in creation, yet which never demand to be taken too seriously.

To understand how the Storybook Style materialized as the court jester among 1920s home styles, we must look back several hundred years, to the eighteenth-century English movement known as the Picturesque. In modern usage, the adjective "picturesque" refers to something having the qualities of a picture or a painting, or having a charming or quaint appearance—in itself a fair summary of a Storybook Style home. But to an architect of 1750, Picturesque design meant much more: it was an entirely new approach whose aim was to elicit an emotional rather than a rational response.

The term Picturesque was originally applied to an English school of landscape design that arose in reaction to the rigidly formalistic landscape schemes typified by gardens such as those at Versailles. While the latter sought to assert man's dominance over nature, the Picturesque school espoused naturalistic compositions meant to mimic nature herself.

The most famous garden of the Picturesque school was Stourhead, completed in 1744, which was in fact literally based upon an idyllic landscape painting by Claude Lorrain done a century earlier. Stourhead, which still exists, features a series of curious structures, including an obelisk, a temple, and a grotto, carefully disposed along a meandering two-mile-long path to create a series of idyllic Picturesque vistas.

By the mid-1700s, the Picturesque movement began to influence architecture as well. It soon formed a countercurrent to the prevailing architectural mode of the time, nowadays known by the oxymoronic label Romantic Classicism. Spurred on by Nicholas Revett's publication of *Antiquities of Athens* in 1762, Romantic Classicism drew heavily on the newly rediscovered elements of Greek Classical architecture; it favored simple geometric forms, smooth surfaces with an absence of relief, and a frequently Brobdingnagian scale.

While the discipline and clarity of Romantic Classic architecture reflected a desire to build rationally for an increasingly enlightened world, the appeal of the Picturesque was emotional rather than intellectual—the Mr. Hyde to Romantic Classicism's Jekyll, as it were. Picturesque architects were willing to draw on a wide variety of past styles and periods for effect, and were especially fascinated by structures that fell outside the rubric of Classical architecture. Medieval fortifications, French farmhouses, English peasant cottages, and Middle Eastern temples all provided grist for Picturesque composition.

To understand the appeal of such anti-Classical designs, we must consider the context of the early eighteenth century. The world now stood on the verge of the first industrial age, with the architectural catalog of all Classical antiquity growing ever more complete. Yet paradoxically, this new wealth of knowledge seemed to leave Romantic Classic architects ever more constrained by academic formulas with little room for variation.

That Picturesque design offered an occasional respite from the rigors of Romantic Classicism is borne out by the fact that court-favored architects such as John Nash (1752–1835), who normally practiced well within the boundaries of Romantic Classicism, also produced some of the most theatrically Picturesque buildings extant.

It is notable that serious architects such as Nash—much less his aristocratic clientele—could be inspired by vernacular buildings, which had seldom been of interest to the world of architecture. Vernacular styles had evolved from need and suitability, not from adherence to any recognized style, and it was an entirely new development to perceive aesthetic value in them. To be sure, whatever charm architects or the aristocracy might have found in these buildings would hardly have been apparent to their daily inhabitants.

Nevertheless, perhaps in reaction to the restrictive doctrines of Romantic Classicism, or perhaps merely out of wistfulness for pre-industrial times, the architecture of the ordinary took on great interest for the first time. As early as 1783, Marie Antoinette had directed her architects to construct a mock-medieval French *hameau* in Versailles park (fig. 1). There, outfitted with a milkmaid dress and a silver milk-pail, the Queen of France dabbled in being bourgeois—at least until the French Revolution could give her a more authentic experience.

In Britain, reproduction "castles" soon appeared on the scene, driven by a growing nostalgia for the days of the medieval monarchy. Among the earliest examples of such shammery is the castellated "ruin" found in Hagley Park at Worcestershire, designed by the architect-squire Sanderson Miller in 1747. Miller, who built similar mock-ruins for a number of his friends, was not alone in his taste for contrived decay; similar structures—built mainly as garden follies —were soon appearing throughout Britain.

Exotic architecture also figured prominently in the Picturesque sensibility. In England, the Prince of Wales commissioned several increasingly eccentric remodels of his farmhouse at Brighton. The first, in 1787, turned the modest country dwelling into a fairly routine Classical pavilion, but a second, in 1797, redecorated the interior in the "Chinese" style then in fashion. In 1807, the architect Humphrey

Repton was retained to rework the building yet again, this time in what was known as the "Hindoo" or Indian style. Repton's plan apparently didn't impress the Prince, but another scheme by Nash did. Accordingly, in 1815, Brighton Pavilion was transformed into a Middle Eastern mirage of onion domes and minarets (fig. 2) that still presents an incongruous silhouette against the dour Brighton sky.

In 1811, Nash constructed a group of nine cottages on the estate of J. S. Harford in Blaise, Gloucestershire (fig. 3), each of differing design. Eschewing the usual Romantic Classic tenets, Nash based his designs upon medieval English peasant dwellings, borrowing vernacular elements such as thatch roofs and irregular massing to lend an air of antiquity to each composition.

The 1814 publication of Sir Walter Scott's first novel, *Waverly*, further aroused interest in Britain's medieval past, especially in the castellated and vernacular architecture of the time. Accordingly, in 1823, King George IV remodeled the stylistic jumble of Windsor Castle into a cohesive, mock-medieval Picturesque mansion in which the only genuine medieval portions were ironically submerged. Balmoral, a relatively modest retreat built in the late 1830s, received the same royal treatment beginning in 1853, becoming an even more celebrated example of what architectural-historian Henry-Russell Hitchcock has bluntly dubbed the "fake castle" mode.

Fake-castle building was not confined to Britain, however. In Germany, the intermittently lucid, Wagner-obsessed King of Bavaria, Ludwig II, trumped all others with his colossal homage to Wagnerian opera, Neuschwanstein (fig. 4). This was a fantastical "medieval" castle designed by Eduard Riedel (1815–1885) and begun only in 1869. Neuschwanstein's exterior was not completed until 1881, and the interiors still later, with much of the design work done by the operatic backdrop-painter C. Jank. Just a few decades hence, this literal connection to theatre would reappear in the Storybook Style.

THE REVIVAL OF HAND CRAFTSMANSHIP

During the eighteenth and early nineteenth centuries, even as Romantic Classic architects were busily replicating Greek temples, profound technical and social changes were taking place. The Industrial Revolution, so humbly portended by Thomas Newcomen's wheezing steam engine of 1711, had irrevocably affected the nature of industry, economy, and social structure. By the middle of the nineteenth century, it was poised to revolutionize aesthetics as well.

The year 1851 saw one of the watershed events of this first industrial age. It was the Great Exposition of the Works of Industry of All Nations, held in London's Hyde Park and housed in the celebrated Crystal Palace. The latter was a vast, 1,851-foot-long hall of iron and glass designed, not by an architect, but by the sixth Duke of Devonshire's gardener,

1. In 1783, Marie Antoinette began creating an idealized French village for her amusement on the grounds of Versailles. Her architect, Richard Mique, modeled the buildings upon farming complexes in Normandy's Caux region. The *hameau* marked one of the earliest appreciations of the architecture of the ordinary. (Photo by Sandra McLean)

2. In 1815, after a number of prior remodels that he apparently found insufficiently exotic, the Prince of Wales engaged architect John Nash to redesign the royal pavilion at Brighton. The result was this improbably exotic blend of Indian, Saracenic, and Chinese design. Nash was a man of flexible tastes, and had no compunctions about designing classically in one instance and exotically in another. (Photo by Sue Edmonds)

3. In 1811, Nash designed a group of nine cottages on the estate of J. S. Harford in Blaise, Gloucestershire, each different, but all using vernacular devices such as thatch roofing and irregular composition. The elite had discovered that vernacular styles were worthy of study, admiration, and even emulation. (Photo courtesy of Harthill Art Associates Inc.)

4. Ludwig II of Bavaria was obsessed with the operas of Richard Wagner, and the castle of Neuschwanstein, begun only in 1869, was his homage to Wagnerian romanticism. Despite its modernity—the exterior was not completed until 1881—it has long formed the public's ideal of what a real castle should look like. No doubt for this reason, Walt Disney chose Neuschwanstein as a model for Sleeping Beauty's Castle, the centerpiece of the original Disneyland that opened in Anaheim, California, in 1955. (Photo by Steve Whittaker)

5. In 1859, William Morris collaborated with architect Philip Webb on the design of his home at Bexley Heath. Known simply as the Red House, its vernacular palette of materials and direct expression of function helped reawaken interest in simplicity and hand craftsmanship as an antidote to the rampant eclecticism of Victorian design. (Photo by Ted Bosley)

Joseph Paxton (1803–1865). Assembled out of some 23,000 identical cast-iron trusses and 900,000 square feet of standard-sized glass sheets, it was erected in the astoundingly brief span of nine months and quickly gained worldwide fame as the first major prefabricated structure.

While the Crystal Palace promptly become a paradigm of modernity, the goods displayed inside were another matter. For the most part, a Victorian eclecticism of the most confused sort ran rampant over the items displayed, whether stoves, clocks, or furniture. Stylistic periods were combined not merely within rooms, but within objects, yielding a hodgepodge of conflicting themes. To an enthusiastic public, the Exhibition was nothing less than a cracking good show; to social critics, on the other hand, it was a harbinger of aesthetic and social decline.

By the time of the Great Exhibition, it was already apparent that the phenomenal advances of the Industrial Revolution had come at a dreadful cost. The wholesale transfer of labor from cottage to mill quickly brought about ghastly living conditions in the crowded, smoke-palled cities of the new industrial age. And while industry had put a vast range of goods within reach of the working class, it had simultaneously deprived them of the niceties of clean air, clean water, and decent housing.

For some, the antidote to these woes lay in a return to the past. Among the most influential exponents of such thinking was the architect Augustus Welby Northmore Pugin (1812–1852). In his *Contrasts*, published in 1836, Pugin argued for the primacy of Gothic architecture. His aim was not merely to extoll the Gothic as an applied style, as others had already done, but rather to inspire a complete revival of the Gothic building methods of the Middle Ages.

In 1849, the English critic John Ruskin (1819–1900) published *The Seven Lamps of Architecture*, in which he argued that art is based upon national and individual integrity and morality. Two years later he amplified this view in *The Stones of Venice* (1851), which argued that Venice's Gothic architecture represented domestic virtue, while its Renaissance works reflected corruption. Ruskin likewise applied his equation of aesthetics and morality to the problems of the machine age, insisting that the decline of art and architecture was a reflection of the ugliness and waste of modern industry.

As for the famed Crystal Palace, Ruskin dismissed it as "a greenhouse larger than ever a greenhouse was built before." Paxton's superlative engineering feats alone did not qualify it as architecture, Ruskin insisted, since a true architect must not merely be a good builder but ". . . must, somehow, tell us a fairy tale out of his head beside all this, else we cannot praise him for his imagination."

Influenced by Ruskin's writings, the poet and artist William Morris (1834–1896) also sought to revive the medieval decorative arts by returning to the craft methods of the Middle Ages. In 1859, Morris collaborated with architect Philip

Webb on the design of his home at Bexley Heath, known simply as the Red House (fig. 5). Recalling the directness and simplicity of fourteenth-century monastic architecture, the Red House proved enormously influential among architects disillusioned with Victorian eclecticism.

In 1861, in reaction to the growing debauchery of aesthetics by industrialism, Morris founded what would become the famed decorating firm of Morris and Company. In 1891, he published his influential *Notes from Nowhere*, in which he contrasted the poetry and beauty of the Middle Ages with the ugliness of the industrial age. Ironically, Morris's insistence on hand craftsmanship ultimately served only to limit his products to the wealthy few who could afford to ignore the economies of mass production.

Pugin, Ruskin, and Morris were each eloquent in condemning the coarseness and materialism brought on by the Industrial Revolution. Although all three romanticized the medieval past to a degree bordering on delusion, their appeals for a return to a simpler, craft-based society nevertheless had a profound impact on the aesthetic of the dawning twentieth century. The Arts and Crafts Movement they helped found would ultimately prevail over the rudderless aesthetic of the Victorian age.

For the balance of the nineteenth century, however, the worst nightmares of Pugin, Ruskin, and Morris did in fact come true. Art and architecture sank ever deeper into the morass of eclecticism, spurred on by the widespread availability of machine-made ornament of every description. Clearly, there would be no retreat to a pre-industrial age. Yet by and by, the spread of the Arts and Crafts Movement would bring an appreciation for hand craftsmanship back under the rubric of fine architecture. This in turn would inspire later American architects—including those of the Storybook Style—to stave off, for a few more decades, the arrival of European Modernism, with its attendant deification of the machine.

Curiously, in light of its later tendencies, some of the germinal works of Modernism in Europe drew far more from Picturesque attitudes than from any machine aesthetic. From the final decade of the nineteenth century through the first two decades of the twentieth, a number of movements which broke away from "'traditional" architecture presaged the arrival of Modernism, yet also held some portent for the unfettered aesthetic of the Storybook Style.

MODERNIST MISCHIEF

The earliest of these movements was Art Nouveau, which arose in the final years of the nineteenth century. Its landmarks, found mainly in Belgium and France, featured a delicate and naturalistic ornament of a kind never seen in Classical architecture. The prototype of the genre was the Tassel house in Brussels, designed in 1892 by the architect Victor Horta (fig. 6). In this groundbreaking design, Horta

5

conjured up an organic idiom of tendril-like metal decoration that snaked its way up columns and along staircases, while similar vegetal motifs slithered across floors and walls.

The singular decorative style of Art Nouveau, like that of the Arts and Crafts Movement in England, depended on such a high degree of artistry that its mainstream adoption was never likely. Flourishing for barely a decade, it appeared as a brief but spectacular aberration in the transitional styles of the century's end. Its significance to the Storybook Style lay not so much in letter as in spirit: as one of the first proto-Modern styles to throw off the rigid tenets of Romantic Classicism, it freed architects to experiment with shaping and ornamenting structures in exuberant new ways.

A precursor to the more fantastical leanings of the Storybook Style was the intensely personal work of the Catalan architect Antoni Gaudí which, like that of Art Nouveau, shows a decidedly anti-Classical fascination with organically curved elements. While Gaudí's early work was grounded in Spanish medieval architecture, his style grew ever more quirky and original, as evidenced by such remarkable structures as Barcelona's Casa Batlló (fig. 7), completed in 1907. Here Gaudí boldly modeled the building into pulsating, plastic shapes that seem more organic than architectural. Gaudí's work was published in New York as early as 1892, making it likely that these later buildings were well known in the United States by the 1920s.

Gaudí's designs contain recurring themes that remain entirely his own. In the Casa Batlló, the walls writhe and sway as if formed by the action of pounding surf, while superbly crafted ironwork drapes across balcony rails like tangles of seaweed. Most remarkable of all is the building's wildly undulating roofscape, which is decorated with broken bits of colored tile and sprouts a complement of surrealistic chimneys. The inventiveness and outright humor of these forms are remarkably similar to certain later Storybook Style works.

A school of plastic design with equally humorous detailing—though perhaps a bit more Northern European restraint—also arose in Holland around this time. There, during the Teens, a group of architects known as the Amsterdam School began designing masonry buildings characterized by undulating surfaces, highly decorative brickwork, and almost comically phallic imagery. Most notable is the work of Michael de Klerk, whose picturesque compositions—while frequently classified as early Modern—can hardly escape comparison with Storybook Style design. In his Hill and Eigen Haard housing estates (fig. 8), built between 1913 and 1921, de Klerk assembled a most peculiar and evocative array of forms that even the most noted scholars of architecture have found difficult to classify.

After noting the "stage-set-like unreality" of de Klerk's facades, Henry-Russell Hitchcock observed: "Highly imaginative, even whimsical, features of detail . . . give an air of good humor, and even of the outright humorous, that is rare in any other architecture, ancient or modern . . . de Klerk's whimsy is never nightmarish, in the way Gaudí's can be . . ."

In America, meanwhile, architecture was finally moving away from Victorian eclecticism. By the time of Ruskin's death in 1900, the frenetically decorated Victorian styles had held sway for fifty years, progressing through increasingly florid Italianate, Mansard, and Stick-Eastlake modes. The trend culminated in the outrageously bombastic Queen Anne homes of the 1880s, which drew appreciable derision even at the time. In his autobiography, Frank Lloyd Wright recalled the sort of houses he had seen on a walk through the fashionable suburbs of Chicago during the late 1880s:

> High front-steps went straight up to jigger-porches wriggling with turned balusters, squirming with wanton scroll-work . . . all had the murderous corner-tower . . . either rectangular across the corner, round, or octagonal, eventuating above in candlesnuffer roofs, turnip domes or corkscrew spires. I walked along the miles of this expensive mummery, trying to get into the thinking processes of the builders. Failed to get hold of any thinking they had done at all. The forms were utterly meaningless, though apparently much scheming and copying had gone into them.

Such criticism became more vocal as the century drew to a close. After a generation of ornamental excess, the Victorian Age had left a sour taste on many palates.

THE TIDE TURNS

Not surprisingly, the architectural ideals of the dawning century were diametrically opposed to those of the Victorians. There was a resurgent interest in nature and hand craftsmanship inspired by the Arts and Crafts Movement, as well as a demand for simpler floor plans by household advocates who decried the impracticalities of Victorian design. Applied ornament was rejected as a useless vulgarity, and sham finishes such as graining and faux marble were condemned in favor of natural materials used frankly.

As early as the 1880s, the prominent East Coast architectural firm of McKim, Mead & White began experimenting with houses that omitted the usual ornamental encrustations and were clothed in plain shingles instead. By the late '90s, similar houses were already superseding their Victorian brethren. This development, known as the Shingle Style, would prove to be the last hurrah for the East Coast's traditional leading role in residential design. California's population surged during these years, and the greatest opportunities for architectural experimentation naturally followed. By the turn of the century, the West had already assumed the leadership role in residential design.

The California progeny of the Shingle Style, known as the Craftsman Tradition, arose during the years 1890–1910.

6. Architect Victor Horta all but single-handedly set off the brief but remarkably prolific era of Art Nouveau with his Tassel House, built in Brussels in 1892. Horta's fantastical curvilinear ornament drew on nature's organic forms to provide a free-form vocabulary, and helped reintroduce the serpentine curve to architecture.

7. With his otherworldly roofscape for the Casa Batlló in Barcelona, architect Antoni Gaudí gleefully stretched the bounds of architecture's traditional forms and colors. Gaudí's work was well known in the United States by the 1920s, though it surely puzzled many who beheld it. (Photo by Painetworks)

8. The wildly original plastic forms of architect Michael de Klerk's Eigen Haard housing estates seem to defy the rigid confines of their brick construction. De Klerk's singular work helped bring notoriety to Holland's Amsterdam School of the early twentieth century, and gave architects renewed license in the use of both curvature and unapologetic whimsy. (Photo by Peter Roelofs)

9. In 1915, architect Bertram Grosvenor Goodhue rang up the curtain on a new era with his romantic complex of Spanish Baroque buildings for San Diego's Panama-California Exposition. Goodhue's structures, with their tiled plazas, shady arcades, and burbling fountains, seduced Californians into a love affair with Spanish Revival architecture that persists to this day. The Exposition marked a turning point away from the gloomy introspection of the Craftsman era toward the sunny ebullience of European revival styles. This souvenir postcard depicts the South Entrance of the Science and Education Building, with its elaborate Churigurresque entrance portal and gold-leafed tower.

10. French vernacular dwellings are depicted on a postcard of the sort young American soldiers might have sent home from The Great War. The "War To End All Wars" provided many young Americans their first—and often only—opportunity to see faraway Europe. Those who survived brought home memories of the charming vernacular buildings of the European countryside, bringing on a proliferation of European revival designs by the 1920s.

More than a style, it was a comprehensive design philosophy whose tenets espoused fine craftsmanship, the forthright use of natural building materials, and the frank expression of structure. Its most famous practitioner was the architect Bernard Maybeck, the son of a woodcarver, and himself a firm believer in the handicrafts. Under Maybeck and other architects such as Irving Gill and the brothers Greene, stained wood and rough stone gradually replaced the gaudily painted millwork of the Victorian era.

THE RISE OF THE BUNGALOW

The early years of the twentieth century also marked the arrival of a modest home style that would shortly come to dominate the mainstream housing market. The word bungalow, a corruption of the Indian *bangla*, meaning house, was first applied to a form of barracks used by the British Army in Colonial India. It eventually came to mean any single-story structure with a low-pitched roof. Around 1905, this ground-hugging form was merged with the tenets of the Craftsman Tradition to produce the Craftsman Bungalow.

Being inexpensive to build as well as philosophically attuned to the era, the Craftsman Bungalow quickly grew popular throughout California. Around 1915, E. W. Stillwell & Co. of Los Angeles published a booklet of house plans entitled *Western Bungalows*, which reiterated the classic Craftsman arguments for simplicity, economy, and harmony with the outdoors. Furthermore, it advised: "It is better to build a small house than to overburden the budget with debt for a larger one. Mere size is a waste of money and human endeavor."

These Craftsman ideals—the use of natural materials, organic planning, and modest scale—would soon be recast in a rather more theatrical form in the homes of the Storybook Style.

THE FORK IN THE ROAD

In 1915, at the zenith of the Craftsman era, came an event that was to change the course of residential architecture. It was San Diego's Panama-California Exposition, held to commemorate the opening of the Panama Canal that year. The Exposition featured a complex of Spanish Baroque buildings designed by the architect Bertram Goodhue that proved enormously popular with fairgoers (fig. 9). With their clay-tiled plazas, cool fountains, and ranges of shady arcades, Goodhue's romantic compositions were literally a world away from the native styles the public had grown used to. They easily outshone the now-moldering Victorians that dominated the landscape, but more important, they also upstaged the comparatively glum aesthetic of the Craftsman Tradition.

Ironically, only one of Goodhue's imposing buildings was built in permanent materials; the rest were mere stage-set-like shells of stucco and lath destined to be razed after the exhibition closed. Despite their ephemeral con-struction, however, the illusion of mass and permanence imparted by the thin stucco finish was stunningly convincing—a fact that wasn't lost on architects and builders of the time. So beloved were these plaster palaces that most were ultimately preserved, and several have since been reconstructed in permanent materials.

The Exposition's effect on California architecture was also more lasting than expected: its idyllic buildings and courts ignited a Californian love affair with the Spanish Revival that continues to this day. By the early '20s this popularity had broadened into a general fascination with European revival styles in general. The stage was now set for the Storybook Style, the most exuberant European revival of all.

PHOTOGRAPHY BRINGS THE WORLD HOME

That Goodhue's authentic and self-assured handling of the Spanish Baroque could appear only decades after the naïve "historical" concoctions of the Victorians points to one of the most powerful influences on architecture during the '20s. By the late nineteenth century, advances in printing had for the first time given architects widespread access to photographs of buildings both monumental and vernacular. The invention of the halftone process in the 1890s gave rise to the publishing of photographs in magazine form, and by the turn of the century architectural trade journals had joined mainstream magazines such as the *National Geographic* in featuring photographs rather than engravings.

Initially, the photographic essays in trade journals focused on domestic architecture; as early as 1898, for example, the *American Architect and Building News* offered a popular series on Colonial-era buildings. By the Teens, portfolios illustrating various European vernacular styles were also widely available, and by the late '20s, magazines such as *Architecture* were publishing portfolios of buildings in Europe and the Middle East. Such documentation immeasurably broadened the architect's grasp of non-native design, and led to renditions of formerly "exotic" styles that became at once more common and more authentic.

THE GREAT WAR INTERVENES

Ironically, it remained for a bleak turn of history to germinate the seeds of the Storybook Style. In Europe, inconclusive warfare had been raging between Germany and the allied nations of Britain and France, among others, since August 1914. During this time, the United States had maintained a tenuous grip on neutrality. However, Germany's declaration of unrestricted submarine warfare on the British, made in an effort to end Britain's control of the seas, finally caused the United States to break off diplomatic relations in February 1917. On April 6, the United States entered the war.

American troops and materiel now flowed across the Atlantic to be consumed in brutal trench warfare along the Western Front, which for the better part of the war remained mired along a line extending from Ostende in the north through San Quentin and down through Luneville in the south. By the signing of the Armistice at Compiegne on November 11, 1918, some ten million lives had been claimed on both sides.

Yet the cataclysm of The Great War, whose outcome served only to precipitate an even greater conflict in the coming years, did leave a legacy of a more positive kind on the American psyche. For the American soldier it was the first—and frequently the only—exposure he would have to the European continent. Inasmuch as few who survived this war ever forgot the experience, it is all but certain that the quaint rural architecture of Flanders, France, and Germany, so different from that of the United States, would remain firmly fixed in every soldier's mind along with less happy memories (fig. 10). By way of The Great War, the culture of Europe had, for the first time, left its imprint on a broad cross-section of young Americans.

THE MAINSTREAM

As the 1920s dawned, the time-tested Bungalow remained by far the most popular home style nationwide. Having shed most of its ancestral Craftsman trappings by the late Teens, it emerged clothed in a more economical stucco finish that earned it a new appellation—California Bungalow (fig. 11). To ward off boredom with the basically predictable Bungalow formula, builders varied minor details such as porch columns, window muntins, bargeboards, and brackets, thereby managing to distinguish each house from its neighbors.

The '20s also saw a resurgence in the Colonial Revival style. The first Colonial craze began in 1876, when the Philadelphia Centennial Exposition reacquainted Americans with the clean-lined, foursquare homes of their New England forebears. This first generation was almost comically naïve, amounting to little more than standard Victorian forms bedecked with Colonial icons such as Classical columns, eagle cartouches, and Palladian windows.

However, authentic Colonial-era houses were among the first to benefit from photographic documention in trade journals. With architects thus tutored, the second-generation Colonials of the early twentieth century were far more authentic than their predecessors, and became a long-running favorite, especially east of the Mississippi.

THE REVIVAL ARRIVAL

Yet it was the charming and exotic Period Revival styles that began to capture the public's imagination at the outset of the Roaring Twenties. The earliest, most popular, and most ingeniously varied of these was the Spanish Revival, whose origins ironically lay not in Spain, but in California's Spanish Colonial architecture. The remnants of Spanish rule in California, long held in contempt, first achieved a degree of appreciation with the restoration of Mission San Carlos

Borroméo del Carmelo (Mission Carmel), begun in 1884 (fig. 12). There followed an enthusiastic campaign to restore the remaining California missions, most of which had lain in ruins for decades. The belated drive to recover California's Spanish heritage soon came to include the haciendas of assorted Spanish land grantees, and a number of these decaying adobes were "restored" to states their masters could only have imagined.

In 1890, San Francisco architect Willis Polk introduced a short-lived but influential magazine called *Architecture News* that featured drawings and written accounts of California mission buildings, further legitimizing what became known as the Mission Style.

In the late '90s, Phoebe Apperson Hearst, the wealthy widow of California mining magnate George Hearst, returned from a European vacation with a whopping enthusiasm for Spanish architecture. She promptly hired architect Julia Morgan to design her a Spanish Revival mansion in rural Livermore, California—an affiliation that eventually won Morgan the commission to design the estate of Phoebe's son, William Randolph Hearst. By 1917, the enormous Mediterranean fantasy that Hearst modestly christened Casa Grande would begin rising from a commanding hilltop at San Simeon (fig. 13).

Still, Spanish Revival architecture remained largely an indulgence of the wealthy until 1915, when Goodhue's spectacular embodiment of the Spanish Baroque at San Diego's Panama-California Exposition sparked a long-running craze for European revival styles in California and eventually nationwide.

ALL COMERS ACCEPTED

The whole range of Spanish Revival subtypes—Mission and Mediterranean, Churriguerresque and Pueblo—was soon joined by reinterpretations of rural French architecture, whose popularity had soared after The Great War, and by an array of medieval and post-medieval English styles known variously as Tudor, Elizabethan, Jacobean, or Half-Timbered.

In the case of tract houses, at least, all of the foregoing remained true to the new century's credo of simplicity. Like their Bungalow competitors, these homes were compactly planned, modest in scale, and typically executed in stucco. There the similarity ends, however, for the Period Revival styles threw off the ascetic attributes of the Craftsman Tradition in favor of a far more exotic vocabulary, whether Spanish, French, or English.

Despite the growing fascination with European precedents among both architects and the public, early Period Revival examples tended to be either clumsily naïve or overly dry and academic, depending on the caliber of the architect or builder. The availability of better reference materials soon helped rectify that situation, and authentically executed

790:—Home of Tom Mix, near Los Angeles, Cal.

11. During the early years of the twentieth century, the woodsy Craftsman Bungalow was a staple of American mainstream housing. In the late Teens, its exterior received a makeover in the guise of stucco—a once rarely used finish whose popularity had soared courtesy of Goodhue's fair buildings for the Panama-California Exposition. The result was known as the California Bungalow, and it quickly became the most popular home style of the 1920s. What the Bungalow lacked in flamboyance, it made up for in economy and practicality, and vast numbers were built throughout the United States. The surprisingly modest example on this souvenir postcard was the home of cowboy star Tom Mix.

12. The restoration of Mission Carmel, begun in 1884, signaled a slow and steady increase in respect for Spanish Colonial architecture, and also marked the beginnings of Spanish Revival (née Mission Revival) architecture in California. By the turn of the century, Spanish Colonial ruins throughout the West were being fervently restored to an idealized state that may never have existed; they have provided boundless architectural inspiration ever since.

SAN CARLOS BORROMEO (CARMEL) MISSION, NEAR MONTEREY, CALIFORNIA, FOUNDED 1770

13. Casa Grande, the palatial residence of newspaper magnate William Randolph Hearst at San Simeon, California, was designed by architect Julia Morgan and begun in 1917. It was the most spectacular evocation of Mediterranean-inspired architecture of its time, and added yet more fuel to the public's fascination with European styles.

Period Revival homes became legion during the '20s. Yet copybook design does not a Storybook house make. It remained for the elements of exaggeration, artifice, and humor to be fused into the Period Revival mixture, in a process that could perhaps only have transpired in one place in America—a city in which a clutch of quaint but well-behaved home styles would be transmogrified into movie-caliber fantasy.

CONSUMMATE ARTIFICE: HOLLYWOOD AND THE STORYBOOK STYLE

Even before the arrival of the film industry, Los Angeles residents had shown a penchant for the venerable. In 1904, brewing magnate Adophus Busch had engaged the expatriate Scottish landscape architect R. G. Fraser to transform a barren arroyo on his Pasadena winter estate into a singular garden dotted with a group of Old World features of the most theatrical kind, including an old mill complete with a waterwheel and stone statuary depicting nursery-rhyme themes. Curious Angelinos flocked to the erstwhile private gardens in such numbers that Busch opened them to the public free of charge in 1905. Busch Gardens (fig. 14) not only became a beloved destination for Sunday outings, but predictibly enough was also tapped as a location for a number of films, including *Pride and Prejudice* and *Robin Hood.*

Given the propensity of Angelinos toward the unusual, it is perhaps inevitable that the epicenter of the Storybook Style, that most theatrical of home styles, lies in the capital of make-believe: Hollywood. The once-sleepy hamlet made its first film in 1911, and by 1913 it had already usurped New York as the motion picture capital of the United States, due largely to a number of bitter patent disputes then raging in the film industry. In 1909, companies holding essential filmmaking patents had formed the Motion Picture Patents Company in an effort to bar unlicensed firms from production and distribution. As a result, many independents moved their operations to Los Angeles—due not only to its ideal year-round climate, but because its proximity to Mexico made for a quick escape in case of injunction.

Here, during the Roaring Twenties, there arose two peculiar conditions that would bring the Storybook Style to fruition. The first had to do with the nature of the film industry itself. By the early 1920s, the star system had already begun to form. While sound motion pictures would not arrive until Al Jolson's *The Jazz Singer* in 1927, there already existed a stable of silent-film stars—Douglas Fairbanks, Mary Pickford, John Gilbert, Lillian Gish, and Clara Bow to name but a few—as well as large numbers of lesser lights. Behind them was an entire cadre of creative and production people. As the studios prospered and these "movie people" grew wealthy, a demand arose for homes that would suitably reflect both the status of the stars and the fantasy embodied in the film industry itself. Unlike the sedate manors of bankers and businessmen, these houses would be fanciful monuments to the pathologically flamboyant.

The second condition was one of logistics. The Los Angeles basin was home to a burgeoning film industry whose craftsmen were already second to none in evoking the appearance of long-gone eras and faraway lands. Hence Hollywood was uniquely qualified to produce homes of the Storybook Style's felicity and originality. No starch-collared East Coast architect could have endowed these houses with such a sense of theater.

As Hollywood flourished in the early '20s, Period Revival homes began to dot the Los Angeles area in growing numbers. Most were relatively sober examples of Spanish Revival, Normandy, or Half-Timber modes; yet tucked among them could now be found isolated outbreaks of Storybook Style madness. The upshot was at once ironic and fitting: Los Angeles, a city renowned for its youth and impermanence, would devise for America the consummate version of instant antiquity.

Perhaps the most literal example of the Storybook Style's Hollywood lineage is the Spadena House (figs. 15, 16). Designed by art director Harry Oliver in 1921 and built for the Willat studio in Culver City to house offices and dressing rooms, the building doubled as a movie set and appeared in a number of silent films of the '20s. It was moved to Beverly Hills in 1934 and has since served as a private residence.

ARCHITECTURE ON-SCREEN

Yet such isolated developments were merely a preview of Hollywood's larger role in the Storybook Style, and would have remained an aberration of the Los Angeles psyche had it not been for another Hollywood product with a far more pervasive influence—the motion picture, which immeasurably broadened the public's exposure to "foreign" culture and thus to foreign architecture. During the '20s, a panoply of films set in exotic locations and bygone eras showcased the same sensibilities behind the entertaining madness of Hollywoodland.

Depictions of the distant, the rare, and the exotic had been central to film almost since its inception. The magic of cinema made it possible to transport audiences not only across geographical distance—whether to London, Paris, or Baghdad—but across time itself. The "period" film became a staple of early directors such as D. W. Griffith and Cecil B. DeMille, and it remained a popular genre precisely because it offered the public an escape from the here-and-now.

Aside from the wealthy and those who had fought in The Great War, few people in the early twentieth century had traveled internationally; fewer still would do so during the Great Depression. Hence, exotic film settings held great fascination for the average moviegoer, who might never have set foot outside his own state, much less outside the United

View in Busch Gardens, Pasadena, Cal.

14. Busch Gardens, created by the millionaire brewer Adolphus Busch and landscape architect R. G. Fraser, opened to the public in 1904. The Gardens featured a number of theatrically Old World structures, such as the Old Mill pictured here. In 1920, the American Legion took over the Gardens' management and instituted a 25-cent admission fee. The Gardens remained open until 1938, when the Busch heirs finally grew weary of maintaining the vast property. They offered it to the City of Pasadena, which declined, also citing maintenance costs. The property was subdivided over subsequent decades, although a number of the original buildings still exist.

THE HOME DESIGNER
and
Garden Beautiful

PUBLISHED BY DIXON AND HILLEN, OAKLAND, CAL.
MARCH
15 cents $1.00 a year

15. This is a stylized rendition of the Spadena House as it appeared on the March 1926 cover of *The Home Designer and Garden Beautiful*, a magazine published by Northern California tract-house architect Walter W. Dixon. Designed by Harry Oliver, art director of the Willat Studio in Culver City, the house had received considerable publicity by the mid-1920s for its theatrically exaggerated look of antiquity.

16. *(Opposite)* The Spadena House returned for an encore in the July 1926 issue of Dixon's magazine, this time with photographs and captions describing its "irregular, crooked and distorted" lines and "old weather-beaten appearance." Thus, a building that began life as a set designer's quirky aberration soon became widely influential among maverick architects in search of new ideas.

All lines in the designs are irregular, crooked and distorted, even the metal bars in the windows are not made straight. All of which, together with color used in painting the house, gives an old weather-beaten appearance.

A NEW HOME WITH AN AGED "OLD WORLD" APPEARANCE

This home was built at Beverley Hills, Los Angeles, California.

JULY, 1926

States, and whose exposure to vernacular European architecture was likely limited to the odd photograph in *National Geographic*.

Accordingly, many classic films of the silent era (not to mention a host of mediocre ones) were set in Europe or the Middle East (fig. 17). Rex Ingram's 1921 film *The Four Horsemen of the Apocalypse*, which made Rudolf Valentino a star, was partly set in Paris and the French countryside. The following year, Valentino appeared in George Melford's *The Sheik*, which clinched his reputation as a heartthrob and also exposed audiences to the most romantic of Middle Eastern settings. Nineteen twenty-three brought a slew of period films set abroad, from *Robin Hood*, starring Douglas Fairbanks Jr., to *The Hunchback of Notre Dame* with Lon Chaney, to Cecil B. DeMille's biblical epic *The Ten Commandments*.

Thanks to such formidable entertainment, weekly movie attendance soared to around 100,000,000 during the '20s—one ticket for nearly every man, woman, and child in the United States. The public thronged theaters, not just to see their favorite stars, but also to experience exotic foreign locales they were unlikely ever to visit in person. Studio executives were quick to capitalize on this fact, and period films with romantic settings remained a Hollywood staple for most of the decade. Classics abound: in 1924, Raoul Walsh gave us *The Thief of Baghdad;* 1925 saw Lon Chaney in *The Phantom of the Opera;* 1926 brought Fred Niblo's colossal production of *Ben-Hur.* In 1927, William Wellman made *Wings*, the story of two young men sent to France to fight in The Great War.

ARCHITECTURE REAL AND IMAGINED

In the early film industry, as in the modern one, economics often dictated that both interiors and exteriors be shot on film stages or studio backlots rather than on actual locations. Hence, by the early 1920s, set designers and carpenters were already proficient at evoking the buildings of many lands and eras; they also became expert at artificially aging materials to capture the appearance of antiquity when required (fig. 18). To help ensure authenticity, studios maintained libraries containing information on a vast range of architectural styles and periods, much of it drawn from the same kinds of photographic portfolios used by architects. The earliest of these, the Universal Studios Research Library, was created for Universal founder Carl Laemmle in 1916. Within a few years, most of the major studios had followed Laemmle's lead and assembled libraries of their own.

The film industry's expertise at evoking the architecture of distant places and times was unwittingly influential on residential architecture. Exotic settings such as those being routinely seen in motion pictures had previously been available only in published photographs, which in turn had been common only since the turn of the century. By the late '20s, however, movie sets—the products of Hollywood's best architectural talents—were on exhibit to a hundred million

Americans a week. Such vast exposure proved far more influential on public taste than any static image could have.

The influence of motion pictures on the public only increased during the Great Depression, when movie theaters were among the few businesses that actually prospered. Films set in exotic locations and viewed in the improbably grand surroundings of the movie palaces allowed moviegoers to escape, however briefly, from the stark economic realities they faced outside.

MINING THE PAST

Throughout the '20s and '30s, architectural-trade magazines remained an invaluable source of vernacular European design, and could be found in the libraries of architects and film studios alike. In 1926, for instance, *Architecture* magazine introduced ". . . A Series of Collections of Photographs Illustrating Various Minor Architectural Details," beginning with a monograph entitled *Dormer Windows.* In 1927, the magazine offered additional monographs on *Stone Masonry Texture, English Chimneys, Textures of Brickwork,* and *Iron Railings,* among others. It followed with *Chimney Tops, Door Hoods, Bay Windows,* and *Cupolas* in 1928, and continued into the mid-'30s with *Window Grilles, French Stonework,* and *Corbels.*

With such exhaustive references at hand, and with a superheated economy providing plenty of commissions, there seemed to be no limit to the fanciful homes architects might conjure up given adequate time and money. America thrived, and so did the Storybook Style: by the latter half of the '20s, it had made the leap from the Los Angeles basin to San Francisco and its environs. There, the work of architects such as William R. Yelland and Carr Jones set a new standard of quality for Storybook design. Yet fate had other plans. Rather than inaugurating an even more promising phase of the Storybook Style, these delightful homes would mark its zenith, and usher in its denouement.

BLACK TUESDAY

On October 29, 1929, the New York stock market crashed, losing a huge fraction of its value overnight and bankrupting countless investors. The Great Depression had begun. At its peak, some sixteen million Americans were out of work—about a third of the labor force. Between 1929 and 1933, the gross national product plunged by some forty-seven percent.

The hardships of the Great Depression led to a widespread disenchantment with American values. By 1931, the nation was careening into a state of economic chaos that the Hoover administration seemed powerless to address. Membership in the Communist Party of the United States reached its all-time peak during these years, as poverty-stricken Americans lost confidence in the democratic system.

Architecture was not immune from this questioning of things American. The Bungalow, which had dominated the

17. A postcard depicting the 1922 production of Elinor Glyn's *Beyond the Rocks,* starring Gloria Swanson and Rudolf Valentino. The set is a "German" tavern; the caption on the reverse of the postcard reads: "Working-up 'atmosphere.' The authoress is telling Gloria a heart-rending story to 'bring the tears' appropriate to the impending 'shot.' An accompanying tinkle of 'sob' music does its part in helping on the emotional climax."

Rodolph Valentino, Gloria Swanson and Elinor Glyn, Paramount Studios, Hollywood.

Building a "set" at the Metro Studios, Hollywood.

18. This souvenir postcard shows carpenters constructing a film set on the interior stages at Metro Studios in Hollywood, circa 1920. The "Western town" set is being constructed within a larger period set in order to conserve stage space. The art directors responsible for set design were not only familiar with period architecture but were also expert at patinating materials to produce a convincing illusion of age, as this example would likely demand. At least one art director, Harry Oliver of the Willat Studio, went on to design a number of early Storybook Style landmarks in Los Angeles, including the Tam O'Shanter Restaurant and the Spadena House.

residential landscape for over a quarter century, had already been waning in popularity by the mid '20s, and the Great Depression ended its reign for good. The Colonial Revival style had remained a favorite east of the Mississippi throughout the '20s; yet by the early '30s its Yankee virtues no longer seemed so appealing. In place of these home-grown designs, the public became increasingly enamored of exotic styles based on European precedents. So it was that the bleakest years of the Great Depression ironically yielded some of the most exuberant tract homes of the twentieth century.

Builders were quick to capitalize on the public's appetite for escape. Prior to the Crash, small tracts of Storybook Style homes bearing evocative names such as Normandy Gardens, Normandy Towers, and Stonehenge had already been underway in former Bungalow strongholds such as Oakland and Los Angeles, and construction of such houses continued through the worst years of the Great Depression. The Storybook Style's arrival into the mainstream was all but certified when Sears, Roebuck & Co. offered a medievalized English cottage in its catalog of 1931, complete with catslide roof and rubble-stone trim around the entrance.

The fact that Americans happily bought into such outlandish Continental fantasies vividly illustrates the escapist mindset of the Great Depression era. Nevertheless, this period marked the beginning of a slow but steady decline in the design quality of Storybook Style homes, due less to the scarcity of money and resources than to the inevitable dilution that occurs when a style achieves mass popularity. Builders became increasingly parsimonious with Storybook hallmarks such as staggered brick, rubble stone, wrought iron, and carved wood. In lieu of such creative embellishments, they resorted to broad-brush emblematic devices such as turrets and dovecotes to lend a vaguely European charm. As the '30s wore on, it became increasingly difficult to distinguish these houses from their academic Period Revival contemporaries.

In any case, by the early '30s, a more glamorous competitor loomed on the horizon. In 1925, the Exposition Internationale des Arts Décoratifs et Industriels Modernes held in Paris had introduced the world to an entirely new vocabulary of decoration. Although it took a number of years for this new wave to reach the United States, by the early '30s many forward-looking architects were adopting the style we now call Art Deco. In stark contrast to the Storybook Style's rustic idiom of stone, brick, and stucco, Art Deco employed a gleaming palette of materials—glass block, stainless steel, ceramic tile, and vitrolite—that rendered its precursors instantly obsolete (fig. 19).

In the commercial areas of larger cities, the antiquarian aesthetic of the '20s was rapidly displaced by Art Deco's crisp geometry and futuristic sheen—a transition especially evident in trend-conscious building types such as movie theaters and retail stores. While Art Deco ultimately met with little success in single-family homes, its widespread appearance midway through the Great Depression did have a larger effect on the architectural zeitgeist. In Europe, the antihistoric International Style had already won the day, although its primacy would quickly suffer under the Nazis. By the mid-'30s, the collective consciousness of the United States, too, began to look toward the future rather than the past.

The reasons for this sea change are complex, but owe much to the growing public optimism engendered by Franklin Roosevelt's New Deal. Between Roosevelt's inauguration in January 1933 and the close of 1934, the new administration managed to push through a flurry of legislation aimed at economic recovery and social reform. In 1935 came the founding of the Works Progress Administration, whose aim was to employ the jobless on useful public projects. Before its abolition in 1943, the WPA would construct some 116,000 buildings nationwide, most of them in the futuristic Art Deco-based variant known as Streamline Moderne.

The New Deal had left its imprint; more and more Americans now placed their faith in a dazzling urban future instead of an imaginary rural past. This change was objectified at the New York World's Fair of 1939, where the General Motors Futurama displayed a sparkling miniature City of Tomorrow, replete with streamlined cars and gleaming towers. Here, beneath the gathering clouds of war, the past became passé, and the storybook was closed.

19. *(Opposite)* By the early '30s, the futuristic sheen of Art Deco, with its electrifying new vocabulary of ornament and its gleaming palette of stainless steel, glass, and vitrolite, was quickly rendering revival styles obsolete. Under the stewardship of Franklin Roosevelt and his New Deal, Americans had chosen to embrace the future; Art Deco and its derivative style, Streamline Moderne, pointed the way. Seen here is the lobby of Miller & Pfleuger's Art Deco masterpiece, the Paramount Theater, constructed in Oakland in 1931.

THE CURTAIN RISES

The basic scarcity of Storybook Style works, along with historical accounts that are often either sketchy or overly fanciful, make it difficult to plumb the early history of the style with academic precision; nevertheless, construction dates and both written and anecdotal evidence clearly fix its origins to the Los Angeles vicinity during the early 1920s.

In fact, a curious harbinger of the Storybook Style appeared in Los Angeles as early as 1919. Known as Studio Court, it was built by a Danish immigrant named Einar Cortsen Petersen, a muralist and painter whose work once graced the interiors of some twenty buildings in downtown Los Angeles.

Petersen's quaint and modestly scaled design for Studio Court was meant to recall the feeling of his Danish home town, Abeltoft, from which he emigrated in 1912. Studio Court is entered through a streetfront portal building leading into a long central courtyard; four cottages, originally intended as studios for artists and artisans, line the court on two sides. By all rights, it is among the earliest examples of the Storybook Style; yet Petersen's direct personal links to northern Europe make Studio Court an anomaly among later Storybook works. From a historical perspective, its appearance is akin to that of a man who wanders onstage by accident and is mistaken for the opening act.

The hand of studio art director Harry Oliver, architect of the aforementioned Spadena House, also appears in another of the earliest and best-documented examples of the Storybook Style's Hollywood origins: the Tam O'Shanter Restaurant, built by Lawrence Frank in 1922 in a then-bucolic Los Angeles outskirt called Atwater Village. Frank, who had cofounded Van de Kamp's Holland Dutch Bakers with Theodore Van de Kamp in 1915, had considered opening a restaurant for some years. He saw his opportunity in 1921, after his father-in-law showed him a corner lot he had bought

the previous year on what is now Los Feliz Boulevard, at the time a largely undeveloped stretch of road linking Hollywood and Glendale.

The pragmatic Frank recognized that the site's remoteness would require an attention-getting building in order to attract customers. Accordingly, he sought out Oliver, who had already designed bakery stores in the form of Dutch windmills for the Van de Kamp firm, and gave him free rein to come up with something unique. The result, unsurprisingly, was pure theater: an exaggerated "medieval" cottage with half-timbering, rough-cast stucco, and a spectacular sway-backed roofscape clad in seawave-patterned wood shingle. Oliver borrowed many of his set-design tricks to give the Tam O'Shanter a venerable look: the building's walls were purposely framed off-plumb, and its plasterwork was distressed to resemble aged masonry. Exposed timbers were first charred in a local lumberyard's incinerator and then wire-brushed to produce the effect of great age.

Originally called Montgomery's Country Inn, the struggling restaurant was renamed Montgomery's Chanticleer Inn in 1923. The same year, Oliver was retained to design an addition containing two dining rooms. The new structure, in the same vein as the original, was set off by a fine, stout turret of the sort that would become a Storybook Style hallmark during the next decade. In 1925, the restaurant was reworked yet again, this time with a Scottish theme and a name to match: Tam O'Shanter, after the poem by Robert Burns. This latest incarnation proved successful, and the restaurant has prospered down to the present.

Oliver's original corner building for the Tam O'Shanter was removed in 1930 to provide parking (the restaurant had just instituted drive-in service, reputedly the nation's first), leaving only his turreted 1923 addition. A major remodel was undertaken in 1938, but Oliver was not involved. After mov-

20. Einar Petersen's Studio Court of 1919 proved an early and perhaps unwitting preview of the rambunctious designs to come. With its strident half-timbering, staggered shake roofs, and crude batten doors, the complex was more daringly rustic than the drily academic revival styles of the time. Though Petersen had in mind to capture the essence of his Danish home town of Abeltoft and not the medieval vernaculars of England or France, he soon found himself at the forefront of the Storybook era.

ing to the Fox Studios in the mid-'20s, and having been nominated for Academy Awards for art direction in 1929 and 1930, he inexplicably gave up his burgeoning Hollywood career in the early '30s and moved to the California desert.

Yet another remodel of the Tam O'Shanter in 1968 largely obliterated the last traces of Oliver's design, leaving the turret the sole vestige of the building's ramshackle character. Still, the owners have apparently found its original Storybook flavor enough of an asset to attempt the modern half-timbered rendition seen today.

The story of the Tam O'Shanter is typical of the manner in which Storybook Style buildings appeared sporadically throughout the Los Angeles basin during the early '20s. For the most part, these early buildings were the isolated products of independent thinkers; each reflects its owner's singular ideas, and each has a colorful story to match.

22. The lovingly crafted front door of the Spadena House is composed of odd-shaped wooden slabs with their edges "eased" or rounded over to give them a timeworn appearance. The doorbell is precisely that—a bell beside the door.

23. These shutters on the facade of the Spadena House transform a mundane detail into a new form of self-expression. Note also the tottering chimney and stovepipe, and the deliberately ramshackle porch roofs.

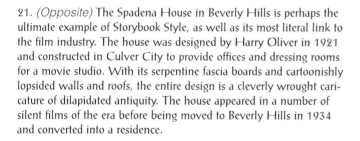

21. (Opposite) The Spadena House in Beverly Hills is perhaps the ultimate example of Storybook Style, as well as its most literal link to the film industry. The house was designed by Harry Oliver in 1921 and constructed in Culver City to provide offices and dressing rooms for a movie studio. With its serpentine fascia boards and cartoonishly lopsided walls and roofs, the entire design is a cleverly wrought caricature of dilapidated antiquity. The house appeared in a number of silent films of the era before being moved to Beverly Hills in 1934 and converted into a residence.

24. (Right) Dormers, which in medieval times merely provided access to the loft of a farmhouse via an external ladder, evolved into windows after the adoption of interior stairs made lofts more convenient for sleeping. Thereafter, they became prominent and highly varied features, especially in vernacular French design. In Storybook Style homes, dormers are generally small-scaled in keeping with the modest scale of the homes, and indeed are sometimes entirely decorative. Front-gabled or hipped dormers of the type common in rural France compete with shed-roofed dormers in the rural English manner, the latter often in the broad "dustpan" configuration. This dormer on the Spadena House rides the swells of Harry Oliver's remarkable roofscape like a rowboat at sea; behind it a most curious chimney seems to be melting in the Southern California heat.

25. A promotional postcard showing the Tam O'Shanter, then known as Mongomery's Chanticleer Inn, as it appeared around 1923.

27. The Tam O'Shanter Restaurant, direct descendant of Harry Oliver's epoch-making building and now a beloved Los Angeles landmark, as it looks today. Despite much modification, it retains the quintessential qualities of all Storybook Style work: a timeless sense of joy in its own creation, and the priceless ability to make people smile.

26. The Tam O'Shanter during the 1930s, when patrons could dine al fresco in the shadow of Harry Oliver's remarkable turret.

28. Every house has a story, and Pasadena's Babcock House has an especially poignant one. Architect Everett Phipps Babcock was a native New Yorker who practiced in Tacoma and Portland before arriving in Pasadena in 1923. Babcock reportedly worked briefly with the noted architect Wallace Neff before establishing his own practice. In 1926, he built himself a combined home and office that amply showcased his mastery of Storybook design. Just two years later, Babcock underwent a routine tonsillectomy, developed complications, and died at the age of fifty-five.

29. In the Babcock living room, a paneled bay with square-leaded panes recalls a common feature of Elizabethan manor houses. The entry windows glimpsed through the archway rotate the muntin pattern into the lozenge shape more commonly associated with "Olde English" designs.

Although the terms Tudor, Elizabethan, Jacobean, and Half-Timbered are often used casually to describe medieval and post-medieval, English-inspired architecture, the terms represent distinct characteristics. The term Tudor refers to English architecture of the first half of the sixteenth century, a period spanning the reigns of the Tudor monarchs Henry VII, Henry VIII, Edward VI, and Mary I. The style is an outgrowth of earlier English Gothic architecture, and features square-headed mullioned windows and openings topped by the familiar four-centered or Tudor arch. Other common Tudor hallmarks include brickwork combined with half-timbering, steep pinnacled gables, a great interior hall lit by oriels or bay windows placed at one or both ends, and large, multiple-flue chimneys used in a decorative manner. Perhaps the quintessential examples of Tudor architecture are found in various colleges of Oxford and Cambridge Universities.

Elizabethan architecture harks from the reign of Elizabeth I (1558–1603), a prosperous and enlightened era that fostered many of England's great manor houses. Architecture of the period is characterized by more rational planning, a diminished emphasis on the medieval "great hall," a greatly expanded use of glass and, where building stone was scarce, a florid use of half-timbering as exterior decoration. The Jacobean style, whose name refers to the reign of England's James I (1603–1625), represents an early phase of the English Renaissance; it forms the transition between Elizabethan architecture and the later Renaissance style introduced by English architects such as Inigo Jones. The corruption "Jacobethan" has also been used to describe late nineteenth- and early twentieth-century English revival styles that were loosely derived from the Elizabethan and Jacobean eras.

The term "half-timbered" is commonly applied to any structure that imitates medieval or post-medieval timber framing with wattle-and-daub or plaster infill; however, it more properly refers to a building technique and not a style.

30. In an alcove off the living room, a window with an interior bifold shutter affords a discreet view of visitors arriving at the front door.

31. Superb bronze door hardware complements the home's medieval theme. The hollow spiral motif is one frequently found in Storybook and Revival Style homes of the '20s.

33. *(Opposite)* The "parrot gate" leads from the foyer to a covered terrace; a simple clay-tile floor continues through the passage, softening the transition between indoors and out. The gate is exquisitely crafted of wrought iron, an accent material prized by Storybook architects for its irregular, hand-worked appearance. Few materials express their hand-crafted quality as directly—the artisan's hammer blows are always evident on the work, frozen in time.

Traditional wrought-iron work is made by heating and hammering a special kind of malleable iron. After the variously shaped elements have been formed, they are joined by welding, riveting, or collaring. Man's use of wrought iron predates recorded history. Prior to 1500 B.C., the Egyptians were refining iron in pits, and its use was already well documented by biblical times—Genesis: IV:22 mentions iron-cutting instruments. In A.D. 1293, the Spanish introduced the Catalan Forge; its use of a crucible with an air blast dramatically increased efficiency and placed Spain at the forefront of the wrought-iron crafts. In contrast, cast iron wasn't developed until around 1350, nor did it see widespread use until the late 1700s.

During the Victorian era, decorative wrought iron was largely supplanted by cast iron, which was more readily mass-produced without sacrificing the florid ornament popular during those years. At the beginning of the twentieth century, the Craftsman Tradition brought medieval crafts such as wrought iron back into vogue, although relatively little use was made of iron in mainstream Craftsman architecture. With the burgeoning popularity of the Spanish Revival after 1915, however, the wrought-iron crafts entered a renaissance. The widespread availability of photographic portfolios featuring vernacular Mediterranean architecture inspired an increasingly lavish use of decorative ironwork in the Spanish manner. Long-dormant ironworking and forging techniques such as piercing and hammer-welding were resuscitated for the elaborate grillework and railings demanded by Spanish Revival design. By the close of The Great War, the revival of ironwork had grown to include vernacular English and French designs as well.

Storybook Style architecture featured some of the most artistic uses of wrought iron since medieval times, and includes far more variety than the usual grilles and railings. Delicate strap hinges and locksets for doors and gates, weathervanes, window boxes, downspout straps, and lighting fixtures all made graceful and often witty use of this ancient craft. Coming upon such details is one of the joys of exploring a Storybook Style gem.

32. A trio of stylish ladies converse over tea in this stained-glass vignette in the living-room window of the Babcock residence.

34. Simple materials lovingly detailed are a hallmark of Storybook design, and the Babcock house contains a wealth of them. In the foyer, massive corbeled beams are distressed to mimic the tooling marks of hand-adzing. They are combined with beautifully crafted wrought-iron work and richly patinated clay tile to produce an effect that speaks with simple eloquence.

35. A freestanding turret set far back on the property provides the tantalizing focal point for this court of Storybook cottages in Los Angeles. Known locally as the Disney Court for its resemblance to the background art in that studio's 1937 legendary film *Snow White and the Seven Dwarfs*, it actually predates that film by a decade. In this case, it's more likely that art imitates life: given the court's proximity to Disney's erstwhile Hyperion Avenue studios just a short walk away, its structures may well have inspired Disney's background artists of the '30s. With delightful serendipity, the court's original telephone prefix was Ivanhoe, and its builder one Robert Sherwood.

36. The owner of the Santa Monica Lumber Company built this medievalized residence for himself in 1923. No doubt due to his access to quality building materials, no effort was spared in the detailing of the house, inside or out. Handcrafted doors, leaded and stained-glass windows, and superb hardware all serve to carry out the Storybook theme. The unusually stout turret in this design encompasses not only the entry, but a small portion of the living room as well.

37. In an unusual plan arrangement, the living room projects halfway into the turret; the top of its vaulted ceiling is visible at the upper left. The pointed arch of the front door is echoed not only in the two leaded-glass windows, but also in the front door peek-a-boo.

38. A massive front-door lockset of bronze in an unusual lever-handle design immediately sets a tone of quality and substance. Note the builder's improvised modification of the filigree to clear a peg in the massive oak door.

39. Pegged oak-plank floors, leaded windows, and an especially fine vaulted and beamed ceiling are nicely set off by lighting fixtures of hammered copper. The stained-glass vignette of a knight on horse-back visible in the leaded front window provides a finishing touch to the home's medieval theme.

40. Distressed battens with oak pegs decorate the superb front door with its double-crossbuck motif. The heavy wooden band or "kick plate" across the bottom is typical of medieval door construction, as this area was especially subject to wear. The peek-a-boo is guarded by a grille of spiral wrought-iron bars, behind which is a tiny beveled glass door.

41. Colored leaded glass and a sill of clay tile distinguish this tiny window in the foyer.

42. An effervescent mixture of stucco and stone instantly draws the eye to this good-humored Pasadena cottage. Its design ably combines three frequent Storybook features—rolled eaves, jerkinhead gables, and a facade extended into low wing walls—with one rarely seen one: an exterior fireplace serving the courtyard.

43. Dating from the mid-'20s, this rambling apartment house provides a touch of Alsace to its North Hollywood setting. The simple plank shutters, protective awnings above the doorways, and sharp distinction between upper and lower stories are characteristic of French Alsatian vernacular architecture, as is the pattern of half-timbering or *colombage*, in which heretofore functional diagonal elements doubled for decoration. The building's authentically aged look is reinforced by carefully irregular composition suggesting organic growth over time—a common Storybook theme.

44. A diminutive pair of towers flank an entrance portal in this Long Beach home dating from 1928, mimicking the drawbridge in a medieval castle. The house has an appropriate fairy story to go along with it: local lore holds that it was built as a husband's gift to his new bride; before the house was completed, however, she discovered that her beloved had already been unfaithful to her. Needless to say, she never occupied it.

45. These windows play more tricks of scale: refer to the general view of the house to gauge their actual size as compared to the front door, and then note their remarkable effectiveness in making the miniature circular towers appear more plausibly castle-like.

46. In keeping with the house's provenance, this miniature crenellated balcony (more properly called a mirador) seems an ideal place from which to soliloquize on the risks of infidelity. In fact, its scale is so small that it could barely contain a few potted plants, let alone a brokenhearted Romeo.

47. Common brick, clinker brick, and stucco combine to produce an arrestingly textured entrance to this Santa Monica home dating from the late 1920s. The circular brick porch cleverly echoes the round-arched door, while the spiky lantern above it provides a counterpoint to the soft curving forms. The meandering transition from masonry to stucco below the dominant gable is a classic Storybook device evoking the picturesquely crumbling facades of many a venerable Old World structure.

48. The crowning feature of this Long Beach cottage is its original "seawave" roof, which has miraculously survived the assault of both fire ordinances and roofing contractors. With its rolled eaves, lovingly crafted shingles, and exceptionally prominent "eyebrow" dormer, it is among the best-preserved examples of the art of Storybook roof-building.

Shingles and shakes are the most common roof materials seen on Storybook Style homes. Shingles (which differ from shakes in being sawn rather than split) date back to medieval times, when they were often cut from the sapwood of species such as oak, beech, and chestnut, the heartwood being reserved for framing timbers. Storybook Style builders treated shingles and shakes—both modestly-priced materials—with refreshing creativity, installing them in a host of delightful patterns meant to evoke the naïve rural architecture of medieval times. The butt ends of shingles were purposely misaligned or placed on a bias, while the spacing of courses was varied either regularly or randomly. Roofing contractors specialized in offset or undulating patterns with names such as "stagger" and "'sea-wave."

In a final medievalizing flourish, some shingle roofs adapted the rural French practice of capping the hips and ridges with a row of clay barrel tiles.

The level of skill exhibited in such roofing work is truly remarkable: shingles meant to emulate thatch were carefully wrapped over rolled eaves, or puckered around eyebrow windows as bark grows around a knothole. Lamentably, due to haphazard workmanship, replacement roofs seldom achieve the original standard of quality.

After Storybook styles entered the housing mainstream following the Great Depression, shrinking construction budgets curtailed much of these whimsical roof details. Seldom could builders indulge in artful imitations such as rolled eaves to suggest thatch, let alone employ costly materials such as slate. Tar-and-gravel roofs appeared, especially on the later mock-castle cottages with their stucco crenellations. Yet where wood shingles persisted, builders stubbornly maintained the rollicking shingle patterns of earlier times. They are sometimes all that remains to distinguish these houses from their straitlaced revival cousins.

49. *(Opposite)* Certainly the largest and possibly the most exuberant example of multi-unit Storybook Style buildings is the imposing Gaytonia Apartments, begun by William Gayton in 1929. King Arthur himself might have blushed at its profusion of parapets, turrets, and ramparts. That the building manages to maintain these high spirits from basement to roof is doubly impressive, considering it was caught half-finished in the midst of the Crash of 1929. Gayton apparently remained unfazed by the economic downturn, and duly completed his self-named monument in the early years of the Great Depression.

While the architectural motifs above the Gaytonia's entrance might appear festive to the modern eye, they would have been rather more forbidding in medieval times. The series of corbels that support the projecting parapets are collectively known as machicolation, and originally served to dissuade enemies from scaling the walls during an attack. The deep recesses in the machicolation could also connect to apertures in the rampart above, allowing missiles or boiling oil to be dropped on the heads of unfortunate attackers.

Like the majority of Storybook buildings, the Gaytonia is finished in stucco, a simple mixture of sand, cement or lime, and water. Stucco's history is both long and dignified. The ancient Greeks applied it over rough stone to get a smooth surface that could be decorated; the Romans mixed it with marble chips to obtain a brilliant interior finish. The magnificent frescoes of the Renaissance were painted onto a form of wet stucco. It remains the finish of choice in sun-scorched Mediterranean lands, where it far outlasts wood.

In the United States, however, stucco was used only infrequently prior to the 1890s. It appeared in the earliest half-timbered buildings of the Colonies—based directly on Medieval English prototypes—where it provided a layer of weather protection over brick or stone infill placed between the half-timbering, or else was mixed directly with wood reinforcement in the construction system known as "wattle and daub." This construction was quickly superseded by the more durable and weathertight horizontal wood siding. Throughout the Colonial era, such siding or wood shingles remained the most common exterior finishes in the North, with brick being more typical in the humid South. As the nation grew westward during the Victorian era, wood remained the choice of builders.

Beginning in 1884 with the restoration of Mission Carmel, a newfound appreciation for the Spanish Colonial architecture of the West and Southwest helped reintroduce the chaste and economical stucco finish. A few clumsily tentative Mission Revival buildings executed in stucco had already appeared by the late 1890s as the Victorian craving for profuse decoration waned.

However, it was the wildly popular Spanish Baroque buildings of San Diego's Panama-California Exposition of 1915 that recaptured stucco's place alongside the wood siding and shingles of the Craftsman Tradition. It was soon back on the palette of forward-looking (or more precisely, backward-looking) architects and builders, who soon realized that, unlike wood finishes, stucco was cheap, went up quickly, and could create a wide range of architectural effects.

Architects and builders first exploited stucco's ability to create false mass in these early Spanish Revival designs, thanks to the paradoxical need to make a modern lightweight material—wood framing—resemble an ancient and heavy one—adobe. By the 1840s, traditional post-and-beam construction had already given way to "balloon framing," a system of light wooden members essentially like the one in use today.

Alas, the walls of balloon-framed buildings looked much thinner and less substantial than their post-and-beam predecessors—a fact that helped earn the new system its derogatory name. Builders learned to compensate for this flimsy appearance by using non-structural framing called "furring" to produce the massive walls, arches and deep reveals demanded by the Spanish Revival. This lightweight framing was in turn covered with building paper and a reinforcing mesh, and stucco was troweled onto it in three successively smoother coats over a period of days.

In the case of the Gaytonia, stucco on wooden furring is convincingly employed to imitate massive battlements, corbels, Gothic arches, and even half timbering: the "wood" you see at upper right is actually cleverly executed in colored stucco. Builders of the 1920s in general became remarkably adept at creating the illusion of mass necessary to many popular styles, but it was in Storybook designs, with their predilection for unusual shapes and aged finishes, that stucco craftsmanship found its zenith.

50. Hollywoodland developer S. H. Woodruff leans to the plow at the dedication of the Hollywoodland sign in 1923. With its fifty-foot-high letters sprinkled with thousands of electric lamp bulbs, the sign quickly outgrew its original advertising purpose to become a Los Angeles landmark, and has since become a worldwide symbol of the film industry.

HOLLYWOODLAND

An early enclave of Storybook Style homes lies in the curious subdivision known as Hollywoodland, located in the hills northwest of Los Angeles. In 1923, developers S. H. Woodruff and Tracy Shoults purchased some five hundred acres of greasewood and oak nestled at the foot of Mt. Lee, just above the town of Hollywood. Here they laid out picturesque winding streets lined with steep hillside building lots ranging in price from $2,500 to $55,000.

Among the earliest structures built at Hollywoodland were the tract's asymmetical pair of entrance pylons, built of rusticated stone quarried from the hills nearby. The pylons were originally to have been fitted with gates and provided with a full-time guard, much as in today's "gated communities," although the latter features never materialized. Gates or no, the picturesquely medieval design of the pylons has earned them registered landmark status with the City of Los Angeles.

To advertise their development, Woodruff and Shoults modestly constructed a fifty-foot-high, five hundred-foot-long electric sign spelling out HOLLYWOODLAND just below the crest of Mt. Lee. Originally built of telephone poles, pipe, and sheet metal, and fitted with several thousand forty-watt lamp bulbs, the sign has become the tract's most enduring legacy.

Unlike the more ostentatious subdivisions of Beverly Hills and Pasadena, Hollywoodland's written advertisements emphasized both the quaintness of its steep setting and the quirkiness of its home styles. Woodruff and Shoults required new homes in the development to be built in "French Normandy, Tudor English, Mediterranean and Spanish styles," a good indication of the status and popularity of Period Revival architecture during the '20s. There appears to have been no restriction as to the authenticity of these styles, however, and a number of home designs stretched the prescribed bounds well into Storybook territory.

Woodruff employed an entire cadre of publicity men, whom he referred to as his "assistant directors," to keep Hollywoodland in the public eye. From the outset, the developers were successful in attracting a wealthy clientele to Hollywoodland. Among the tract's most celebrated residents were the actors Bela Lugosi, Humphrey Bogart, and Gloria Swanson; announcer Lowell Thomas, and, not least, comedy writer Felix Adler, author of many of The Three Stooges two-reeler comedies for Columbia Pictures. The renowned cellist Efrem Zimbalist, Sr. also made his home in Hollywoodland, as did the gangster Bugsy Siegel.

Hollywoodland's dramatic setting lent itself to some appropriately theatrical home designs, most of them in flamboyant Mediterranean or Norman modes. As befits the later pattern of their construction nationwide, the tract's Storybook Style residences are scattered singly throughout—the product, even by Hollywood standards, of slightly eccentric thinking. These houses tend to be more modest in scale, as for example the cottage of actor Humphrey Bogart, which clings to a steep finger of land girded on three sides by a snaking roadway; their siting also favors shady dells rather than the hilltop-crowning sites of their Mediterranean brethren.

Following the onset of the Great Depression in 1929, Woodward and Shoults were forced to curtail their ambitious development plans for Hollywoodland. Many streets that had been planned were never graded, and a few that had already been graded were left unpaved. Maintenance of the Hollywoodland sign was discontinued; thanks to storms and vandalism, the huge structure rapidly decayed, and by 1939 some portions had collapsed. In 1944, the M. H. Sherman Company, successor to Woodward and Shoults, deeded the tract's remaining undeveloped area to the City of Los Angeles, and the land was incorporated into Griffith Park. In 1949, the Hollywood Chamber of Commerce demolished the sign's final four letters, restoring it to read simply "Hollywood." It was the birth of an American icon, but the end of a developer's dream.

51. A worker clings to the Hollywoodland sign's "D." Each letter was constructed from telephone poles, steel pipe, wire, and sheet metal. The sign gained notoriety in 1932 when a despondent English actress named Peg Entwhistle, then staying with her uncle in Hollywoodland, jumped to her death from the letter "H." The sign had long since fallen into disrepair when the final four letters were removed in 1949, as part of a restoration by the Hollywood Chamber of Commerce.

52. One of the rustic-stone gateposts at the entrance of Hollywood-land, among the first structures Woodruff and Shoults built for their new subdivision on the slopes of Mt. Lee. Constructed of "Hollywoodland granite" quarried from the hills nearby, they were originally to be fitted with gates and a full-time guard. Neither materialized.

53. A new residence rises in the then-barren hills of Hollywoodland. The tract's covenants required homes to be designed in one of several European revival styles, and designers and builders made full use of this license, arriving at eclectic combinations that its developers might never have expected. While this example is relatively low-key, its rubble stone chimney, jerkinhead gables, and sea-wave shingles nevertheless land it squarely in Storybook territory.

HOLLYWOODLAND

*A DELIGHTFUL
RESIDENTIAL DISTRICT*

. . . The Hills of Hollywoodland—
Thirty minutes from downtown Los
Angeles—Five minutes from the center of Hollywood, offer splendid home-
sites for those who love the *Freedom
of the Hills* . . . . With Griffith Park
on the East, Beautiful Lake Hollywood on the West, and Mulholland
Highway traversing the crests of its
scenic vantage points Hollywoodland
is indeed the Ideal residential district.

54. As the gigantic Hollywoodland sign will attest, Woodruff and
Shoults were consummate publicity men in the finest tradition of
the '20s. Hollywoodland's advertising took a more subtle approach;
this image evokes the new tract as a place for those who love "the
freedom of the hills."

English home of Mr. and Mrs. Paul E. Thilo

Interesting types of architecture as expressed in the Hills of Hollywoodland

An interesting Norman-French Chateau

55. Two new Hollywoodland homes in the English and French Norman styles were featured in a sumptuous brochure that also sang the praises of the tract's then-bucolic setting—advertised at the time as being "Thirty minutes from downtown Los Angeles—five minutes from the center of Hollywood." Today, the town of Hollywood is contiguous with greater Los Angeles, yet Hollywoodland itself has nevertheless managed to retain the idyllic quality first envisioned by Woodruff and Shoults.

107:—HILLSIDE HOMES IN HOLLYWOODLAND, HOLLYWOOD, CALIFORNIA.

43497

56. A postcard of Hollywoodland dating from the late '20s, showing the development's precipitous setting. The Hollywoodland sign is barely visible in the upper right corner.

57. White Tower was the name originally given this Hollywoodland home with its imposingly crenellated square tower. Built in 1924 by designer-builder A. E. Crist, the house was a wedding gift to a daughter of the Pantages family of theater fame. It was renamed Ivory Tower by a witty subsequent owner with a penchant for collecting books. The current owner, a film production designer, has added many interesting details in keeping with the home's unique character.

58. The living room of Ivory Tower boasts an unusual elliptical-arched plaster ceiling in lieu of the more common Storybook vault-and-beam arrangement. The magnificent 1901 Bechstein grand piano in the background was a gift to Lady Sylvia Ashley from her husband, actor Clark Gable, who reportedly spied it in a show window at Harrod's of London and purchased it on the spot.

59. In contrast to the bright and airy living room, the intimate, book-lined study at Ivory Tower presents a cozy retreat. The series of tile reliefs on the room's massive fireplace are titled "The New World," and came from molds made by the Moravian Pottery and Tile Works of Doylestown, Pennsylvania. The series includes the figures of Christopher Columbus and the Spanish monarchs Ferdinand and Isabella, along with Columbus's three ships.

60. A superb wrought-iron lantern spans the entrance gate at Ivory Tower. The lantern is a modern addition by the present owner, yet is fully in keeping with the home's medieval spirit. It was crafted by a master blacksmith who had restored the ironwork in a number of churches in his native Czechoslovakia before emigrating to the United States.

61. This relief of a glowering face transforms the archway of the entry porch into a gaping mouth. Added to Ivory Tower by the present owner, it is a copy of one he found on a building near Rome's Spanish Steps.

62. A shady Hollywoodland glen is the setting for this true Hansel and Gretel cottage dating from the early 1930s. In the best Storybook tradition, it combines half-timbering, rubble stone walls and chimney, and a seawave-patterned roof with rolled eaves and jerkinhead gables to produce just the right tone of droll dilapidation.

63. Actor Humphrey Bogart called this Hollywoodland cottage home from 1938 to 1940. Designed by Evander Hoven and completed in 1926, its front door is reached via a drawbridge slung on suitably massive chains, now charmingly overgrown with ivy. A 1997 fire destroyed the home's wood shingle seawave roof, along with much of the interior. A local fire ordinance prohibited the reinstallation of wood shingles, and while the present composition-shingle roof is a laudable attempt to maintain the home's original flavor, it cannot compete with the texture of the original.

64. A flower-draped arbor gives onto the walled courtyard of this secluded Hollywoodland home dating from the mid-'20s. Half-timbering, stone trim, rolled eaves, and seawave shingles provide a classic Storybook palette whose feigned antiquity ironically defies the passage of time.

65. Note the carefully distressed half-timbering and intentionally "crumbling" stucco at the home's entrance. In Storybook Style homes, the lumber used for false half-timbering (virtually none was structural) was frequently distressed with rasps or gouges to produce a time-worn appearance; art director/architect Harry Oliver even favored having timbers charred in an incinerator and then wire-brushed to achieve a suitably ancient look.

The crumbled-stucco technique involved affixing a masonry veneer onto a select area of wall and then holding the stucco back from its edges in a ragged shape, revealing an illusory patch of stone or brick from which the stucco appears to have fallen off. This overt bit of shammery is especially derivative of film sets which, like the vast majority of Storybook homes, are generally framed entirely in wood yet deftly imitate masonry buildings of all kinds.

66. A dovecote graces the turret of this Hollywoodland "cottage" once owned by actress Gloria Swanson. Though diminutive in appearance, the house actually rises (or more properly, sinks) to a height of four stories at the rear thanks to its precipitous site. Turrets, like many Storybook Style design features, were inspired by medieval and post-medieval vernacular and defensive structures. Vast numbers of Americans were stationed in Europe during the years of The Great War; many of these were future architects, contractors, and clients who, upon their return, were inspired to include the details of European vernacular architecture in their work.

The prototypes for the various turret forms seen in Storybook Style architecture include not only the circular towers of European defensive architecture, as might be assumed, but also a more diminutive structure common to the French countryside—the dovecote. The practice of rearing pigeons in dovecotes dates back to Roman times; however, the earliest surviving examples are circular towers dating from the sixteenth century. Pigeons were prized for their meat and eggs, but above all for the valuable fertilizer gleaned from their droppings. By the eighteenth century there were some 42,000 dovecotes in France. Based on round, rectangular, or even hexagonal ground plans, these were substantial, free-standing buildings unto themselves, often standing several stories tall. Many of the turrets seen on Storybook homes were inspired by such structures, and include some form of decorative dovecote as a reminder of this heritage.

67. The turrets of most Storybook houses accommodate either an exterior porch or an interior foyer. While the ascending windows of this unusual example mischievously suggest that it contains a winding staircase, the space is in fact merely occupied by a closet.

51

68. *(Opposite)* This is the gatekeeper's residence at Wolf's Lair, the rambling Hollywoodland mansion built by Milton "Bud" Wolf, and later occupied by renowned cellist Efrem Zimbalist, Sr. While the main house is a rather more ponderous Norman Revival-style work dating from the mid-'20s, architect John Lautner gave this little building dating from the 1950s a lighter touch more typical of early Hollywoodland designs. The turret with its rubble-stone base features a pair of sham dovecotes—one at the eave line, and another on the spire—while the projecting bay with its Gothic tracery is supported on medieval machicolation. Ironically, Lautner was best known for his ultramodern Hollywoodland homes of the postwar years; this commission appears to have been a lark.

THE NEXT ACT

By the mid-'20s, architecture featuring broad and often humorously exaggerated "medieval" detailing had made the leap from Southern California to the San Francisco Bay Area. As early as 1924, the San Francisco firm of Sidney and Noble Newsom designed the Henshaw residence in Piedmont, California, a wealthy suburb of Oakland, in an exaggerated vernacular style. Reputedly based on Marie Antoinette's *hameau* on the grounds of the Palace of Versailles, the home's design indicates a growing fascination with the more theatrical aspects of vernacular architecture beyond the Los Angeles area.

While a number of Northern California practitioners occasionally dabbled in the Storybook genre, the most consistent oeuvre of Storybook architecture comes down to us through two singular architects who, despite disparate academic backgrounds, had remarkably similar architectural philosophies. Although it is doubtful that the two men ever met, their Storybook legacies could hardly be more compatible.

William Raymond Yelland was born in Saratoga, California, in 1890, and studied architecture at the University of California at Berkeley under the prominent Beaux-Arts master John Galen Howard; he graduated with a B.S. in architecture in 1913. Yelland was stationed in France during World War I, and came away greatly impressed by rural French architecture. He was especially influenced by the houses of the Auvergne region, with their roughly laid stone walls, doors and windows framed with blocks of granite, dovecotes, and steep hip roofs studded with dormers. In 1920, he wrote of a village in Auvergne: "Everywhere there is a strange atmosphere of simplicity and contentment. I am inclined to feel that, partly anyway, the happy informal way of building has affected their lives." The characteristic features of Auvergne, along with an eclectic mix of other French vernacular influences, would become recurring themes in Yelland's work.

By 1924, Yelland had established his own office in Oakland, and was also teaching architecture at Oakland High School. Like his uncle, the locally renowned artist Raymond Dabb Yelland, he drew and painted in his leisure time, and it is not difficult to discern a similar artistic freedom in the fanciful details of his architecture. A student enrolled in Yelland's class in 1928, at the peak of the architect's career, recalled him to be a "free-hand" designer who seldom used hard lines in his work. Indeed, while the architectural working drawings or blueprints of the era were customarily drawn in ink using mechanical drawing instruments, Yelland's drawings appear to be carried out in pencil, and are drawn at least partially freehand.

Yelland was fascinated by the irregularity of vernacular buildings, and was especially given to emphasizing their quaint and curious details in his own work. In a Yelland design, roofs sag, corners defy the plumb bob, and bricks are laid helter-skelter in a manner bordering on caricature. Yet he bridled at attempts to classify his work as embodying one style or another.

"If you must have a style," Yelland wrote in a 1927 article in the trade magazine *Architect and Engineer*, "call it rural. That is about as vague a word as I can think of. Every time a man puts his hand down to cut or carve or chisel or build a house, he must express his own self."

Yelland was a great believer in the ancient role of architect as master builder, and in a number of his projects he is known to have completed the interior masonry himself. Nor is it likely that his projects would have approached such a level of craftsmanship and impulsive wit had Yelland not been intimately involved in the details of their physical construction.

Yet this medieval approach to design, along with Yelland's propensity toward the more theatrical elements of vernacular European architecture, did not endear him to the succeeding generation of predominantly Modernist architects. Even fifty years later, when asked how Yelland's work had been regarded during the 1920s, a U.C. Berkeley architecture graduate of the period distastefully summed it up with one word: "Cute."

Carr Jones was born in Watsonville, California, in 1885. Like Yelland, he attended the University of California at Berkeley, but studied mechanical engineering rather than architecture. Around the time he received his degree in 1911, however, he designed and built a simple redwood cottage for his parents in Berkeley, thus beginning a long, colorful, and perhaps unintentional career in what would nowadays be called "design-build contracting."

Virtually alone among Bay Area architects of the '20s, Jones worked largely with recycled materials—brick, slate, timber, scrap steel, and bits of salvaged ornament—all of which he utilized with great ingenuity. With these humble castoffs and his appreciable skills at masonry, joinery, and blacksmithing, he managed to conjure lyrically beautiful homes some three-quarters of a century before the advent of "green architecture." Just where Jones acquired these singular sensibilities, we may never know. There is no doubt, however, that he would have been quite comfortable working in today's climate of environmentally responsible design.

Jones's houses are almost invariably built with massive walls of roughly laid bricks left unfinished to show their natural range of ochre hues. A variety of arched openings enliven his interiors, while massive roof beams of salvaged timber provide dignified drama overhead. Many of his houses, such as the Hermans residence in Oakland, have a curved floor plan embracing a central court.

Unlike Yelland, Jones never traveled to Europe, but was inspired by photos of European vernacular buildings published in books and magazines. While his houses embody numerous classic Storybook characteristics—an aged appearance, serpentine curves, and whimsical details—these elements grow organically from the design rather than being superficially applied. It is a happy result of building in a true medieval vernacular, without undue concern for perfection or perception. Jones chose his materials and designs not because they were fashionable, but because he believed in their absolute fitness for domesticity.

Alas, building in a resolutely personal style brought neither Yelland nor Jones great financial success nor, ultimately, even much recognition during their lifetimes. By the mid-'30s, Revival styles had fallen out of favor, and demand for their idiosyncratic compositions dwindled. Yelland's work accordingly became ever more conventional to suit the temper of the times. Jones, by contrast, continued to build sporadically in his trademark style for the rest of his life.

Both men died in 1966. By that time, the surging tide of Modernism had long since rendered their quirky and personal works unfashionable and largely forgotten. Neither lived to see the flowering of the ecology movement in the early 1970s, nor the 1977 publication of Christopher Alexander's seminal work *A Pattern Language*, which implicitly condemned Modernism's sterility and absence of human interest, and instead espoused precisely the kind of architecture both Yelland and Jones had practiced for a half-century.

While history would shortly conspire against the work of Jones and Yelland, for the balance of the '20s, these two remarkable men would show an increasing allegiance to the medieval tradition of the master builder, and thereby set a new standard for the flourishing Storybook Style.

(Overleaf) 69. Designed by San Francisco architects Sidney and Noble Newsom in 1924, the Fritz Henshaw house in Piedmont, California, is among the earliest and largest Storybook works in the state. Its design was reportedly inspired by Marie Antoinette's medieval *hameau* on the grounds of Versailles, and like that remarkable group of structures, every detail is carefully conceived to further the illusion of antiquity. The tinted stucco finish is patinated to suggest age, while the roof eaves and rake are rolled to suggest medieval thatch. Casement windows with lozenge-shaped muntins complete the bucolic image. Too often, such defining features of Storybook Style homes are lost in misguided attempts at modernization; to the current owner's great credit, these charismatic details have all been carefully preserved.

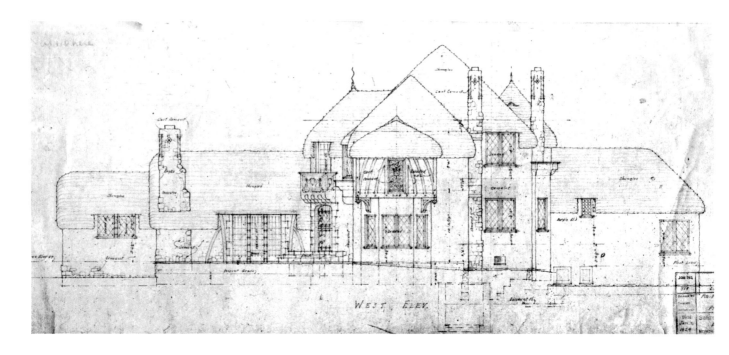

WEST. ELEV.

70. Compared to modern architectural drawings, this front elevation of the Henshaw house is notable for its surprising lack of specificity. Craftsmen of the era were given far greater latitude to carry out the work as they saw fit, so long as it conformed to the general intent of the architects. Hence, the Newsoms provided little more than a schematic representation of the design, with the working out of final details left to the builders.

71. The superb front door features an oak-plank design with an unusually large leaded-glass light. The two-leaved Dutch-door arrangement with its wrought-iron hardware is a rare feature. The artfully patinated stucco work is clearly visible in this view.

58

72. A machicolated balcony with incised reliefs and a pair of leaded-glass doors flanked by rolled eaves make for a texturally rich composition above the home's entrance.

73. A stone-studded chimney is tucked snugly into a corner of the Henshaw house. The rolled eaves extend below the window heads to yield one of the Storybook Style's best imitations of thatch.

75. This tiny structure, built as a gardener's tool shed, delightfully maintains the rolled eaves and whimsical character of the main house.

76. Normandy Village, an eight-unit apartment building a few steps from the University of California at Berkeley, is undoubtedly the magnum opus of William R. Yelland, the master of the Storybook Style in Northern California. The complex was built during 1926–1928 for Yelland's friend, a Great War veteran named Colonel Jack W. Thornburg. Thornburg, a student at the University of California at the time Yelland was commissioned, dreamed of building a unique residence for students and teachers patterned on villages he had seen in Northern France during the war. Normandy Village is the realization of that dream. With its collage of vernacular forms carefully arranged to suggest growth over time, the building is an almost comically exaggerated evocation of rural France, and is vintage Yelland throughout. From the strutting rooster frescoed on the front gable to the outlandish fence with its array of suggestive slats, no detail escaped the architect's finely honed sensibilities.

74. *(Opposite)* While actual thatch roofing was all but unheard of on Storybook Style homes, its appearance was nevertheless frequently imitated. Thatch, from the German word "dach" or roof, is one of the earliest roof materials extant, and remained commonplace until relatively recent times: as late as the eighteenth century, half the houses in France were still roofed with thatch, and in Britain and Ireland there remain an estimated 150,000 thatch-roofed cottages even today.

A thatch roof consists of bundled reeds, heather, or most commonly, straw, which are tightly bound to wooden laths in overlapping horizontal rows, providing both rain protection and excellent insulation. Thatch is not permanent, but must be replaced once every generation; it is also susceptible to fire, a fact that moved many towns to prohibit its use as far back as the Middle Ages. Despite these shortcomings, thatch continued to be employed in rural construction well into the nineteenth century, when noncombustible roofing such as slate and tile became competitive.

Among the middle class, however, thatch roofing had already been considered a mark of poverty for at least two centuries. Only with the coming of the Picturesque movement in the early nineteenth century was its image recast as a quaint rural tradition, as at Blaise Hamlet, where architect John Nash used it in a purposeful revival of rural English tradition.

In America, no tradition of thatch existed—nor is it likely that such a fire hazard would have been tolerated in U.S. cities by the early twentieth century. Storybook Style architects were nevertheless determined to capture thatch's medieval charm. Hence, designs such as the Henshaw house featured "rolled eaves"—boldly rounded roof edges meant to suggest the soft, pillowy eaves and gables seen on traditional thatch-roofed cottages. These roofs were covered with carefully fitted but otherwise conventional wood shingles. In some houses, gutters were built in a few feet above the eave so as not to spoil the rounded edge; in others, they were omitted entirely.

Here, the elaborately detailed rolled eave of the Henshaw house extends down between windows and conforms to the projecting bay window—a demanding piece of workmanship bespeaking the contractor's exceptional skill in Storybook construction.

77. The two-story portal gives onto an intimate courtyard leading to various apartments, no two of which are alike, as well as to a rear garden. An additional apartment building known as Normandy Towers was constructed a few years later, and a rather lackluster postwar interpretation designed by others was built circa the 1950s. It is the original buildings of Normandy Village, however, that remain Yelland's finest composition.

78 A roofed staircase makes a spectacular twisting leap to a second-floor entrance at Normandy Towers, dating from 1929 and also designed by Yelland. The entrance to a ground-floor apartment is sheltered beneath it.

79. A serpentine staircase wends its way up to the circular porch of an upstairs apartment. The steps are once again of colored cement tooled to resemble fitted stone blocks. The steel windows seen at right were an innovation of the '20s used mainly in commercial buildings. While contemporary bungalows and most other tract-home styles retained traditional wood windows, Storybook architects often specified the steel variety, perhaps because their slender frames and muntins bore a passing resemblance to the leaded windows of medieval times.

80. A carved grotesque supports a projecting bay at Normandy Village.

81. A competing array of grotesques peer down from neighboring Normandy Towers.

82. With a simple and ancient palette of materials—brick, tile, wood, iron, and slate—architect-builder Carr Jones conjured inimitable homes of lyrical beauty. An expert mason, Jones acted much like the "master builder" of medieval times—designing, constructing, and even fabricating much of the hardware on his houses. This Oakland residence designed in 1928 boasts his trademark arched entrance and curving walls. The home's roof, with its field of slate edged by clay barrel tiles, recalls a technique common in rural France, where it was used to help prevent leaks at this most susceptible juncture.

Slate roofing is made from a sedimentary stone called schist, which naturally cleaves along well-defined parallel layers; along with thatch, it is a favorite roofing material of vernacular European architecture. Although its use dates back to the Middle Ages, it was largely restricted to the immediate regions in which it was quarried. With the advent of better transportation in the nineteenth century, however, slate quickly made inroads in both Europe and Britain as a replacement for fire-prone thatch.

Jones and other architects prized slate for its natural character and texture—qualities that were further emphasized by the rustic manner in which it was installed. Unlike the carefully squared and aligned slates seen on straight revival-style homes of the era, Storybook Style cottages often boasted randomly sized slates set in exaggeratedly misaligned patterns—the less regular, the better. Many builders also followed the rural European practice of placing the largest slates from random-sized shipments on the lower courses, graduating to smaller pieces toward the ridge.

83. This bell button set in a hand-painted tile is a signature of architect Carr Jones.

84. Another Jones trademark is the glass-filled gable truss seen in many of his living rooms, a startlingly contemporary feature that pre-dates Modernist versions by a generation. The knee braces at the left foreground of the roof framing recall wooden shipbuilding practice. Jones's unreinforced brick construction, while unusually substantial, would never meet modern building codes—a fact that might dampen any enthusiasm toward modern-day versions of his homes. To the owner's great credit, the Hermans residence has been seismically retrofitted with consummate sensitivity to its unique design.

85. *(Opposite)* The living room of the Hermans residence is a vir-tuoso exercise in obtaining high drama from pedestrian materials. As in most of his houses, Jones built the walls of used brick, a product that was neither expensive nor much in demand during the '20s. The massive roof structure is built of salvaged timbers that were wire-brushed, treated with lime, and then waxed. Many metal items are fashioned from castoff Victorian-era hardware, such as the large radiator screen just behind the couch in the background at the left. In short, the house is exemplary of what we would nowadays call "green" architecture. Jones was ahead of his time in other ways as well; the Hermans residence has a still-functioning hybrid radiant heating system using copper tubes embedded in the concrete floor slab and terminating in concealed radiators. What appear to be large windows at the right are actually steel-sash doors that open onto the garden. The archway to the left leads to the study with its stone fireplace.

86. This cozy study with its view of the courtyard is examplary of Jones's unique approach to design. The massive stone fireplace with its crane and kettle was a relic from a cabin that formerly stood on the site; rather than removing it, Jones blended it seamlessly into his own design. The lively and elegant staggered floor pattern is achieved with two sizes of ordinary clay tile.

87. Jones's gift for quirky planning is evident in the dining room of the Hermans residence, where a projecting corner bay, a bedroom door, a corner fireplace, a niche, and a pass-through to the kitchen (the small batten door at the right) all combine in a lively and literally eccentric composition. The roof framing demonstrates Jones's use of the French vernacular technique of "incurving"; note how the mid-height purlin or crosspiece supported by the roof truss is thinner than the upper or lower ones, imparting a subtle curve to the roof sheathing. In rural French practice, incurving served to wedge the roof tiles more tightly against each other, thereby improving water-tightness; perhaps more compelling to Storybook Style builders, it also imparted a dramatic sag to the roof plane.

88. Many of Jones's homes have a curved floor plan embracing a central courtyard. In the Hermans residence, a gallery extends along the inside of the curve, affording access to the outdoors while also connecting the entry, bedrooms, and dining room. In this room, the plain clay flooring gains drama simply by following the curve of the walls. The brick columns supporting the gallery roof are constructed with entasis—the subtle bulging shape that suggests muscles straining to bear a load—an example of Jones's exceptional command of brick masonry. Between the columns are windows with diagonal steel muntins ingeniously suited to follow the curve of the walls.

90. This formidable-looking wrought-iron sconce with its brace of incandescent bulbs is one of a pair that light the curving gallery of the Hermans residence.

89. The lighting fixtures in the Hermans residence are typical of Carr Jones's work, and are designed and proportioned to complement the bold textures of the brick interior walls. This bedroom sconce is among the more delicate examples.

91. Here is yet another variation of wrought-iron sconce in the Hermans residence—this one has a superbly forged spiral pendant.

92. Unexpected details are a keynote in any Carr Jones design. In the Hermans residence, even the basement stairwell holds a surprise: a diminutive pendant fixture of delicate wrought iron.

93. This massive lantern slung on chains illuminates the driveway of the Hermans residence.

94. A classic Carr Jones chimney combining round and rectangular flues embodies both whimsical design and superb craftsmanship.

95. This is the courtyard of the Hermans residence, looking toward the gallery and living room. The columns with their bulging barrel shape or entasis defy the usual constraints of brick construction. The monumental, multi-tiered chimney, with its curious lantern and ornamental plaque of salvaged terra-cotta, could only have come from Jones's hand. Note also the unusual combination of slate and clay barrel tiles on the roof of this elevation—a quirky Jones touch that adds unexpected textural variety.

96. The central courtyard of the Hermans residence includes a fireplace and barbecue with beehive chimney placed just outside the din-
ing-room doors, as well as a whimsical clock recalling those in
European market squares. The herringbone brick paving was left
unmortared, allowing moss to fill the joints. The conically roofed
structure to the right is a tiny breakfast room, yet another Jones trademark.

97. Time stands still in the garden of the Hermans residence, which clings to the edge of a ravine just beyond the home's courtyard. The steps in the foreground lead to a small swimming pool fed by the waterfall seen at the right.

98. With its used brick walls, clerestoried gable, and turreted break-
fast room, Oakland's Smith residence is a veritable catalog of classic
Carr Jones features. The house, dating from 1929, also features
Jones's signature coffered-arch entrance. The three-brick motif visible
above the front dormer at the left approximates a Welsh trigram sym-
bolizing "Truth Against the World"—a fitting motto for an architect
who followed conscience above all else.

100. Many of Jones's homes featured a circular, conical-roof break-fast room such as this one in the Smith residence. Its solid wood ceiling is constructed of tapered vertical staves held together with hoops rather than nails—an innovation which, like many of Jones's unusual building techniques, did not endear him to building inspectors.

101. The front bedroom features a massive roof structure of salvaged timber, another common theme in Jones's work. A small arched alcove facing the street provides a fine spot for reading.

99. *(Opposite)* A round foyer with an unusual brick-domed ceiling forms the home's dramatic hub. The living room, both bedrooms, and a curving stair leading to the garage all open off of this unusual space. A "Jack-and-Jill" or shared bathroom is placed between the bedrooms—an unusual arrangement for the period.

102. This exceptional Oakland home dating from the late 1920s introduces an artificial sag or swayback at the roof ridge to suggest the structural deflection that comes with great age. The concave extension of the main roof over the porch, known as a catslide, demonstrates another version of the technique of incurving. The use of such theatrical aging techniques, as distinct from the mere reproduction of historical forms, furnishes one of the clear distinctions between Storybook Style and straight revival styles. Roofs with rolled eaves, incurved surfaces, and swayback ridges were considerably more difficult to construct than conventional ones, illustrating the importance architects and builders attached to achieving the illusion of age. Great effort and ingenuity went into creating these picturesque and purportedly ancient roofscapes, which remain among the most endearing features of Storybook Style homes. While the architect of this home remains undetermined, its artful composition suggests the hand of William R. Yelland.

103. Gently peaked gables and a pair of regressed dormers enhance a dynamic cascade of roofs on this sprawling Oakland residence dating from the late '20s. The replacement of the original shake roof in kind was a commendable choice, given the home's unusually conspicuous roof surfaces.

104. In this double-barreled rarity in San Francisco, the right turret forms a porch complete with a window, while the left one encloses an entry hall. Storybook architects were positively smitten with the design possibilities inherent in circular turrets, and came up with surprising variations on the theme. Although unusual designs such as this one worked well enough on paper, constructing them often proved quite challenging. While stucco and shingles could easily conform to the required curves, rain gutters could not. In some cases, gutters were laboriously fabricated from short sections joined to produce the required radius; more often, they were simply omitted altogether. The awkward juncture between turret and roof plane also made this area a frequent source of leaks. While the brave designer of this house may have been risking double trouble, he also achieved an admittedly unique result.

(Overleaf) 105. The family of adjectives used to describe Storybook Style homes—whimsical, charming, cute, quaint—all underline the fact that these houses are almost exclusively a small-scale phenomenon; their quirkiness does not translate well to large homes, which are by definition not cute. Occasionally, however, a skillful architect can overcome this tendency, as does this palatial example in San Francisco's tony Presidio Terrace district, designed by William R. Yelland around 1928. Despite the home's large size, Yelland manages to maintain a sense of Storybook quaintness by reducing its massing into discrete sections that appear to have accreted over time. Note, for example, the variation in half-timbering between the two front-facing gables, and its complete absence on the cross gable. The carved gargoyles or grotesques projecting from the circular pavilion at the left are a classic Yelland touch.

106. William R. Yelland designed the rambling, 5,500-square-foot Erskine House in Piedmont, California, during 1925–1926. Like designer-builder Carr Jones, Yelland was a firm believer in the traditional role of architect as master builder, and he reportedly installed much of the interior brickwork himself prior to the building's completion in 1929. The home's third owners recalled their delight at visiting the elderly Yelland at his Berkeley residence in 1962 and being presented with the original blueprints for the house, which remain with it to this day.

107. A German baker reputedly had this Oakland cottage designed to resemble the homes in his native Black Forest. Built in 1929, the house is distinguished by half-timbering, jerkinhead gables, and an underscaled eyebrow dormer, as well as a delightful rose-filled setting.

108. Broad serpentine stairs wend their way up to this whimsical yet sadly neglected firehouse in Oakland, the former home of Engine Co. No. 24. Designed by Robert Edwards of the Oakland Department of Building and Public Works, the firehouse was built in 1927 and features an unusual roof of curved concrete slabs carried on steel trusses. Serpentine copper finials, now obscured by paint, were meant to symbolize fire which "follows along the roofline and leaps into tongues of flame at the gable corners." The area surrounding the large sectional door (a modern replacement) is scored to resemble stone and was originally unpainted. The chimney and gable wall are of clinker brick studded with projecting brickbats, while the lozenge-shaped attic vent is composed of stacked pieces of clay barrel tile.

109. The unusual residential scale of the Oakland Public Library's Montclair branch allowed it to blend in with the modest cottages of this once-bucolic district. Designed and built by contractor C.C. Rosenberry and opened in 1930, the library's swaybacked slate roof and unusual catenary entrance arch bear a notable resemblance to some earlier works of architect W. R. Yelland. The building's design was widely admired, with the April 1930 issue of *Progress* declaring: "Like the Montclair firehouse . . . this new structure is absolutely new in its architectural conception." The library's construction was funded by Chauncey W. Gibson, a wealthy Oakland resident who had made a fortune in the manufacture of carbonic gas for soft drinks. Gibson had no heirs; his only son had died as a child, with his wife following a year later. He thereafter dedicated his life to philanthropic efforts. Described as "gruff in manner, (but) kindly in heart," Gibson joined his wife and son a few months after the library opened, at age 90.

110. This Berkeley, California, landmark by architect Harvey Slocombe has a history as eclectic as its design. Built in 1928 as a chapel for the adjacent undertaking firm of Hull & Durgin ("Berkeley's Pioneer Funeral Directors—Economy Without Cheapness"), it was reportedly modeled on the photograph of a chapel in the native English village of undertaker William Hull's mother. During the '40s and '50s, the erstwhile funeral parlor also served as the venue for over five hundred weddings. By the '70s the building had been remodeled into shops and offices, and for a time also accommodated a Buddhist temple. With its rolled eaves and strangely Balkan belfry, the building commands the instant attention of passing motorists. An especially curious feature is the dense concentration of rubble stone at the building's base, which slowly dissipates to rise almost effervescently up the front face of the tower.

THE LITTLE CHAPEL OF THE FLOWERS (HULL and SONS), BERKELEY, CALIFORNIA

111. The unusual design of Hull's chapel made an eye-catching subject for this promotional postcard dating from the mid-'30s. The reverse side advertised the chapel's availability for weddings.

112. The inimitable William R. Yelland designed this commercial building in Berkeley, California, dating from 1925. Yelland made generous use of cast-stone ornament such as the relief panel framed by the small blind loggia on the upper facade. A typical Storybook motif—the dovecote—appears at the apex of the gable; more unusual is the use of rubbed brick (brick shaped by grinding), visible in the molded string course just above the sign. Shortly after the building's completion, the trade magazine *Architect and Engineer* appraised it as follows: "[Its] style brings to mind many places in the old world—and it has . . . a sense of intimacy, of loving attention to detail, of pleasure in doing something well."

113. An imposing chimney—a fanciful agglomeration of brick and stone—forms the focal point of this Oakland home dating from the early '30s. The facade's relatively simple massing is softened by a combination half-timbering, a corbeled projection above the garage door, a welcoming front porch, and a swaybacked roof.

114. *(Opposite)* San Francisco's densely populated Marina district is the setting for this rare urban example of Storybook design built in the early '30s. Despite its virtually flat facade, the clever arrangement of bow window, chimney, and entrance gable achieves a surprising illusion of depth. The random application of Carmel chalk stone used on the chimney is repeated in the radiating voussoirs of the archway, subtly drawing the eye down to the gated entrance.

Arts & Decoration

DEVOTED TO ARCHITECTURE, BUILDING & INTERIOR DECORATION

"Springtime"

From a Painting by Carl Heck

ARTS & DECORATION PUBLISHING CO. INC.
PUBLISHER — ELTINGE F. WARNER

APRIL, 1929

New York — Paris — London

PRICE: 50 CENTS

115. By the eve of the Great Depression the Storybook Style was recognized from coast to coast. The April 1929 issue of *Arts & Decoration* magazine, published in New York, featured this quintessential turreted cottage on its cover, legitimizing what had once been considered a peculiar aberration of the Southern California psyche.

NOW PLAYING NATIONWIDE

By the mid-1920s, the publication of building photographs such as those of the Tam O'Shanter Restaurant in Los Angeles and the Spadena House in Culver City, both designed by art director Harry Oliver, had exposed the nation to the quirky brand of architecture that had arisen in the nation's movie capital. Naturally, these outlandish buildings did not appeal to everyone's taste; yet for those disposed to the unusual, an awareness of them was enough to inspire further work in the same vein. By plotting construction dates of Storybook designs, the style's spread can be traced from its epicenter in Hollywood to the San Francisco Bay Area of Northern California, and thence into the Pacific Northwest and the rest of the nation.

Rosebush House, located in Millwood, Washington, now a suburb of Spokane, provides an unusual insight into the Storybook Style's gradual evolution outside California. The main house and its elaborate garage were built five years apart, during the early and late 1920s respectively, giving us a pair of historical bookends that document the style's rising influence on residential design of the 1920s.

Waldo Emerson Rosebush was a historian, firearms expert, and patented inventor of some prominence in the Spokane area. He served in the U.S. Army under General John Pershing from 1915 to 1920, and received the Pershing Merit Citation with Purple Heart for his World War I service in Normandy. Rosebush came to Millwood after the war's end, and in 1922 was appointed general manager and treasurer of the Inland Empire Paper Company.

In 1911, Inland Empire had constructed a paper mill in a rural portion of the Spokane Valley known as Woodard Station. The mill prospered, and the community that would eventually become Millwood quickly grew up around it. To ease the demand for housing, the company laid out seventy residential sites for its employees in the early 1920s, provid-ed a $40,000 revolving home-loan fund as an incentive to buyers, and even offered the loan of its steam shovel to dig foundations.

Rosebush was among the first employees to purchase one of these lots, and in 1923 he commissioned Spokane architect Harold Whitehouse to design him a home resembling the thatch-roofed, stucco-clad cottages he had admired during his tour of duty in France. Whitehouse had studied extensively in Europe, as was customary at the time, and responded with a half-timbered stucco cottage with rolled eaves and jerkinhead gables—a charming piece of Normandy Revival design, yet one whose academic dryness kept it firmly under the rubric of Period Revival work.

In 1928, Whitehouse was called upon again, this time to design the Rosebush garage. This was a garage in name only, since it also included a finished basement connected to the main house by an underground tunnel, three horse stalls on the main floor, and servants' quarters upstairs. Beyond its elaborate program, however, the Rosebush garage vividly illustrates the expanding stylistic license that the passage of five short years brought about. Its design shows architect Whitehouse moving beyond the academic Normandy Revival detailing of the residence to include broad medieval themes approaching caricature in the classic Storybook manner: the garage doors are now quite theatrically framed in the form of a castle portal, complete with a false portcullis looming overhead and "windlass chains" dangling from slots at either side. In addition, Whitehouse amended the straightforward idiom of stucco, half timbering, and casement windows he used in the main house to include a rather remarkable ruinlike adjunct of rubble stone with deeply recessed slit windows.

Within less than a decade of its inception in Los Angeles, the liberating tide of the Storybook Style had reached the Pacific Northwest.

116. The main house and garage of paper-mill executive Waldo
Rosebush vividly illustrate the spread of Storybook design nationally
during the 1920s. The main house seen here was built in 1923, and
maintains a relatively sedate idiom of stucco, half-timbering, and
casement windows—fairly routine features of Normandy Revival
homes of the time.

117. This is a lovely if relatively sober design for the entrance to the main house of 1923. While the superb front door and staggered brick paving are suitably medieval, more strident Storybook traits are not yet present. The stucco finish on the walls remains crisply regular, while the half-timbering is applied two-dimensionally and without distressing.

(Overleaf) 118. In contrast to the main house, the garage built just five years later is fairly bursting with Storybook exuberance. By the time it was designed in 1928, Rosebush's architect, Harold Whitehouse, had digressed from the archaeologically correct Normandy vernacular of the earlier building into far more theatrical territory. The garage doors are now guarded by a portcullis quite literally copied from a medieval-castle portal, while an adjunct of rubble stone with deeply recessed slit windows spills ruin-like from the left side.

119. Hovering spikes of the massive wooden portcullis provide a formidable guard for a pendant lamp hanging above the garage's plank doors.

120. The rear veranda of the Rosebush house, where sunlight filters playfully through a vine-covered pergola overhead. In contrast to the home's public facade, the veranda's arches and clay-tile floors suggest an ambience more Mediterranean than Norman. Note the thick wall reveal visible in the triple-arched opening; both the house and garage are built of structural terra-cotta or "hollow tile," a material widely used in commercial buildings of the '20s, but seldom seen in Storybook work. Here, it lends a subtle look of mass and permanence to Whitehouse's design.

121. A delicately wrought amber-glass pendant fixture graces the stairway leading to the garage's upper floor.

122. Milwaukee, Wisconsin, is the setting for this lovely stone cottage, which seems to have materialized bodily from a Currier & Ives print. The eclectic design combines a diminutive, castle-like tower form at the entrance with round-arched windows and a jerkinhead gable, all beautifully executed in buff Wisconsin ashlar (dressed stone).

123. This Chico, California, home dating from the early '30s reveals the creeping influence of Storybook details: catslide roof at the entrance, half-timbering, and a curiously tentative use of random brick in the chimney.

124. The steep catslide roof on this Milwaukee home plunges nearly to the ground, affording easy access for roof-roaming felines. Fine ashlar masonry forms the subtly chamfered entry arch, while randomly placed slabs of ashlar are used to enliven the yellow stock-brick chimney.

125. Polychromed brick reminiscent of vernacular Flemish design brings a sense of lightness and charm to the exterior of this well-executed Seattle home.

126. Spokane's spectacularly ivy-draped Cunningham House was designed by locally prominent architect Randolf Smith and built in 1929. Smith's design includes a number of classic Storybook features—a front entrance opening into a turret, steel windows, and a jerkinhead gable—as well as an anomalous one: a clay-tile roof. Rigid interlocking tiles were not easily applied to the complex roof curvatures often favored by Storybook architects, and were seldom specified. In this instance, the problem was skirted by omitting the turret's customary conical roof. Note also the roughly-troweled stucco, which evidently provides a fine foothold for the local species of ivy.

127. This châteauesque home in Milwaukee features handsome stonework, a fine slate roof, and an abundance of chimneys.

128. Battered walls, a delicately upswept roof, and a deeply recessed front door combine to produce a handsomely proportioned entrance to this Milwaukee residence. The unusual blind window and lantern are used to balance the facade's off-axis composition, while the semicircular porch steps repeat the arched forms of the front door and attic window.

129. Radiating voussoirs of brick draw the eye to the entrance of this home in Milwaukee. The random brick edging of the arch is a variation on the more common rubble-stone theme.

1130. Elegantly curved ashlar masonry makes for an exceptionally suave turret on this Milwaukee residence. The turret's soft circular form is admirably set off by the towering, blade-like chimney that intersects it.

131. Superb masonry distinguishes this powerfully composed residence in Baltimore, Maryland. Here, the ashlar (dressed stone) masonry more typical of East Coast architecture is replaced by rubble stone, yielding an unusually rustic effect. The massive curving lintels above the door and window are each cut from a single stone block.

132. This palatial residence in Washington, D.C., features a superbly confident grouping of turret and chimney whose powerful mass is set off by the delicate filigree of the wrought-iron entrance gate and balcony rail. The clever disposition of brick and stone helps break the powerful composition into discrete units to avoiding an overbearingly monolithic effect. A fine slate roof completes the look of incomparable permanence.

133. Rubble stone, polychromed brick, and salvaged lumber are the materials used in the Asheville, North Carolina, residence of prominent local architect Douglas Ellington, which was begun in the 1930s. Ellington continued to expand the house piecemeal as time, inspiration, and his supply of recycled materials would allow. Happily, the architect's singular creation remains in the Ellington family to this day.

134. The great room of the Ellington house exemplifies the architect's devoted use of recycled material. The ceiling beams were salvaged from a local schoolhouse that was being dismantled, while the granite fireplace on the far wall was built with excess stone from a local building project.

136. Flat slabs of rubble stone again serve to form voussoirs above this doorway arch. The deeply recessed door contains a leaded-glass panel in a lozenge pattern.

135. The dressed-stone surround of the massive fireplace in the Ellington house provides a handsome contrast to the rubble stone of the chimney breast. The band of flooring in front of the cobblestone hearth is simply an ad hoc collection of whole and broken tiles of various shapes and colors.

137. Flat stones were culled from the mason's stockpile and used to create the radiating voussoirs in the arch of this doorway in the Ellington house. Oversize strap hinges and a window with random leading set off the simple plank door.

138. This stained-glass panel from an exterior door of the Ellington house carries the inscription: "Welcome ever smiles, and farewell goes out sighing."

139. Builder Hugh Comstock
came to Carmel, California, to
visit his sister in 1924, and neither he nor the sleepy little
town were quite the same
thereafter. Within the year,
Comstock had met and married
Mayotta Browne, a maker of
locally popular rag dolls known
as Otsy-Totsys, and built a tiny
house nicknamed Gretel in
which she could display them.
A year later, Comstock built
this neighboring cottage known
as Hansel, launching both his
building career and a Carmel
building style that endures
down to the present. (Photo by
Arrol Gellner)

140. Comstock's trademark style, here illustrated by Carmel's Tuck Box retail store of 1926, was reportedly inspired by the illustrations of the noted British painter Arthur Rackham. The Tuck Box's remarkably plastic detailing, along with its use of a local building stone known as "Carmel chalk," has inspired many a Carmel architect since, and has been instrumental in establishing the quaint atmosphere of this seaside tourist destination. (Photo by Arrol Gellner)

ENSEMBLES

While most Storybook Style homes are by nature one-of-a-kind designs, the style also inspired tracts of varying size throughout the nation. Some of these were based on the "bungalow court" pattern that had been popular since the Teens, while others were laid out conventionally. All are noteworthy for the individual creativity of their home designs as well as the collective charm they lend to the streetscape.

The name that stands out in the design of Storybook Style tract homes is that of Oakland-based architect Walter W. Dixon. Born in San Francisco in 1883, Dixon traveled to Normandy to study rural French architecture, and from 1922 to 1926 published a magazine entitled *The Home Designer and Garden Beautiful* which, not incidentally, featured a large number of his own designs. He also published a popular book of plans for small homes, and established a plan service to provide builders with stock blueprints; these designs were used in states as distant as Florida. In his homes, Dixon sought to include, as he put it, "the little features that suggest and give the character and feeling of the larger, more expensive home."

Dixon's designs for small houses were used in three of the most notable Storybook tracts extant, all of them in the Oakland area, and all three showing considerable innovation in planning and construction.

The earliest of these tracts was Normandy Gardens, constructed between 1925 and 1926 by contractor R. C. Hillen, who eventually built some three hundred Dixon-designed homes in the Oakland area. Hillen's axial site plan for Normandy Gardens focused on a central site occupied by a large duplex dwelling known as The Castle, with single-family homes surrounding it on either side. Hillen reportedly based this ingenious layout on that of a medieval Norman village, with its manor house surrounded by cottages—a romantic notion with the practical benefit of allowing him to combine single-family and multi-family dwellings in an architecturally cohesive manner.

In 1926, an Arkansas-born developer named Christopher Columbus Howard again chose Dixon's designs for Stonehenge, a unique tract of Storybook homes in Alameda, California. Stonehenge's layout is basically that of a "bungalow court," in which a group of attached dwellings surround a central garden court in a U-shape. However, Howard cleverly modified this concept by substituting detached, two-story cottages with rear-facing garages accessed by a service road, and complemented Dixon's half-timbered medieval designs with a superb landscaping scheme focusing on a central fountain.

In the late '20s, R. C. Hillen's former construction superintendent, Ernest W. Urch, began his own building business under the registered trademark "Builder of Modest Mansions." Urch once again called upon Dixon's plans for a unique Storybook tract on Oakland's Ross Street. This time, it was not the site planning but the infrastructure that stood out. Electrical and phone cables were laid underground—a very early example of this practice—and the street itself was paved in concrete rather than asphalt. Rolled curbs and handsome cast-iron lamp standards provided the finishing touches.

Although a number of other contractors built homes in the Ross Street tract, it is the work of Dixon and Urch that shines with a sense of architectural unity leavened by joyful variations in detail. Lamentably, a portion of the tract was destroyed by freeway construction during the 1960s, making

it difficult to appreciate the original effect of this pioneering neighborhood design.

Today's tract developers could learn much from these neighborhoods. In contrast to the pseudo-Classical pomposity of much of today's housing, Storybook Style tracts are light-hearted in conception and unfailingly friendly in scale—attributes that make them both universally cherished and impeccably maintained by their residents.

141. Stonehenge is the whimsical name of this cottage tract developed by Christopher Columbus Howard in Alameda, California. Howard began planning Stonehenge in 1926, loosely basing it on the popular pattern then known as a "bungalow court." Using the designs of master Storybook architect W. W. Dixon, he began the first house in 1927, and completed the project in 1929.

143. A burbling fountain forms the centerpiece for the idyllic court-yard at Stonehenge. Despite the advent of the Great Depression, the development's concept was so successful that Howard purchased an adjoining parcel and built a virtually identical project called Stoneleigh in 1931. This was followed by the final phase, Lincoln Court, in 1941. Together they comprise twenty-seven houses forming one of the most remarkable enclaves of Storybook homes extant.

142. *(Opposite)* Stonehenge's two-story homes are capped with heavy shakes and liberally trimmed in the same Carmel-chalk stone that forms the entrance arch. Automobile access is by a narrow driveway tucked unobtrusively behind the homes—a feature that eliminates garages from the front elevation and allows each house to address the landscaped courtyard.

R. C. HILLEN, BUILDER

DESIGNED BY W. W. DIXON

QUAINTNESS IS SECURED THRU THE USE OF A TOWER

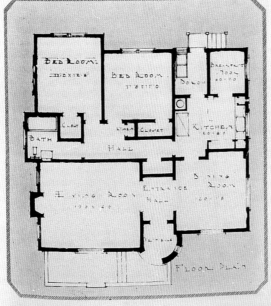

The use of "old world architecture" to give a touch of quaintness and charm to our modern American small home has become quite the thing today, and has a strong appeal to all those who love the old towns of Europe. This home with the half-timbered gable adjoining the tower, with its entrance door to the house, together with the multi-colored shingles laid in irregular, crooked courses, and the bright painted shutters along side the windows, contrasting strongly with light, bright colored walls, makes a very delightful artistic small home.

JUNE, 1926

145. At Oakland's Normandy Gardens, contractor R. C. Hillen created a dazzling array of variations on a mere handful of W. W. Dixon's basic floor plans, conjuring up this delightfully differentiated streetscape.

144. *(Opposite) The Home Designer and Garden Beautiful* was published by architect W. W. Dixon and his frequent collaborator, R. C. Hillen, from 1922 to 1926. Featuring such landmark Storybook designs as the Spadena House and a number of homes by W. R. Yelland, it proved influential in legitimizing the Storybook Style. It also provided excellent advertising for Dixon and Hillen, whose work it frequently featured. This page from the June 1926 issue advocates the turret—here referred to as a tower—as a design element. By way of example, it showcases one of the pair's cottage homes at Normandy Gardens in Oakland. It further opines: "The use of 'old world architecture' . . . has become quite the thing today."

The Norman type of architecture has that quality which immediately draws all eyes. It is picturesque, as witness the house here illustrated. Those turrets and towers arouse one's curiosity. To see them is to become speculative, wondering what stairway would lead up to them and rather anxious to investigate.

AN UNUSUAL DUPLEX HOUSE

*Designed by W. W. Dixon,
Oakland, California*

R. C. HILLEN, BUILDER

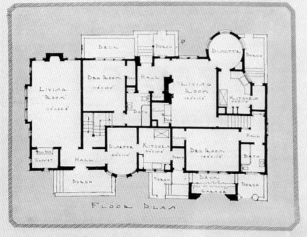

FLOOR PLAN

The French-Gothic ceiling with its heavy oak beams decorated in oils, is a main feature of this living room. The walls are of a composition resembling stone and the floor is of the same material in a darker tone.
Note the very convenient arrangement of the rooms and the generous amount of closet space.

SEPTEMBER, 1926

147. Relatively few Storybook Style homes feature the distinctive crenellated parapet seen in this example at Normandy Gardens. Crenellation, perhaps the defining feature of medieval defensive architecture, originally served to protect a castle's archers from enemy arrows, while still allowing them to fire their bows through the intervening slits. The first revival of crenellation as a stylistic detail dates back to the Picturesque movement of the early 1800s, when English royalty rediscovered the glory of their country's medieval past and engaged their architects to build ever more theatrical castle imitations. A century later, Storybook Style homes once again reignited the public's fascination with castles and the medieval world. The crenellated turrets occasionally seen on Storybook-era homes were rather less successful than their Picturesque predecessors due to their toylike scale. In practical terms, such features also proved dismayingly susceptible to roof leaks and dry rot.

148. This home built by R. C. Hillen in the Dixon-designed tract known as Normandy Gardens dates from 1926; it is among a small number still retaining their original hand-tinted stucco finish. This technique combined complementary shades of colored stucco to produce a patinated finish that would never require repainting. The dovecote—a favorite Storybook motif—appears in two different forms on this house. The one on the gable serves as an attic vent, while the unique elevated model fashioned from a keg is strictly for the birds.

146. *(Opposite)* The Normandy Gardens tract was ingeniously anchored by a duplex home known as The Castle that occupied a jutting peninsular site near the center of the tract. Hillen's intent was that his single-family homes should surround the larger structure just as cottages might surround a medieval manor house.

149. A broad and welcoming set of front steps is the highlight of this tidy cottage in Albany, California. Like many Storybook Style entrances, this one is scaled down to create a sense of intimacy and coziness, while at the same time making the balance of the house look larger. The tiny dormer peeking out from behind the entry roof amplifies the effect. The stack of circular vents at the peak of each gable are most often seen in Spanish Revival architecture, but were also a favorite device of Storybook builders. They are simply lengths of four-inch-diameter clay pipe that extend into the attic.

150. This gem with its incurved porch roof, swaybacked ridges, and leaded windows is one of many charming Storybook cottages in the Berkeley area built by the illustrious "One-Nail MacGregor," a local contractor who reputedly never walked away from a finished house without driving home one last nail for good measure. The sloping or battered walls supporting the entry-porch roof are an unusual feature that admirably serves to draw attention to the entrance. The small projections visible above the entry arch and window are the original attachment points for awnings, which would no doubt have made this facade even more festive.

151. Does this house look familiar? It's identical to the One-Nail MacGregor cottage in figure 150 save for the awning and the choice of shrubbery. The exaggerated swayback roof is clearly visible in this photo, as is the markedly downscaled entrance: note the diminutive height of the arch on the right face of the porch relative to the human-sized one at the front. The two houses stand a block apart in Albany, California.

152. Tucked among Oakland"s ubiquitous rows of bungalows is this
block-long stretch of Storybook gems known as Holy Row. Whether
by coincidence or divine plan, a number of these homes were long
occupied by various local church leaders who, it might be said,
appear to have maintained them quite religiously. Sloping sites produce a tiered effect that further enhances the visual impact of these
quaint homes, which date from the early '30s. Although the designer's name is unknown, the hand of architect W. W. Dixon may be
indicated.

153. An inviting flight of steps leads up to this cheerful cottage on Holy Row. An unusual muntin pattern and Bavarian-flavored scroll-cut bargeboards combine with more familiar elements such as stone window trim and half-timbering to demonstrate the latitude granted to Storybook architects.

A
COMPLETE
LINE
OF
STOCK
PLANS

AN
EXCLUSIVE
SERVICE
FOR
THE
BUILDER

W. W. DIXON

PLAN
SERVICE

PHONE:
GLENCOURT
6978
OAKLAND
CALIFORNIA

PARKWAY
THEATRE BLDG.
1842
PARK
BOULEVARD

154. This advertisement for architect W. W. Dixon's plan service appeared in *The Home Designer and Garden Beautiful.* The editorial portion of the magazine provided Dixon and contractor R. C. Hillen with even better publicity, for the articles often featured their own work.

155. Contractor Ernest W. Urch advertised his Ross Street homes as "Modest Mansions." Architect W. W. Dixon achieved their palatial look through ingenious manipulations of scale. In this example, the miniature machicolations on the projecting gable serve to make the surrounding elements seem more substantial. Complex roof massing with finely spaced shingle courses add to the rambling look. Here, the catslide roof is extended into a stanchion for the driveway gate.

156. *(Opposite)* This is a classic Dixon living room with vaulted ceiling, false beams, and a large steel-sash front window. The random-plank pegged oak floor seen here was an extremely popular pattern during the '20s, and can be found in Period Revival and Storybook Style homes alike. The unusual asymmetric fireplace with its rubble stone trim holds a built-in sconce in the form of a hurricane lamp—another typical Dixon touch.

157. Both flights ascend in this curious staircase arrangement on Ross Street. The stair at the left climbs but a few steps to a rear bedroom, while the other continues on to the second floor. The wrought-iron scrollwork of the handrail echoes the design and finish of the home's original curtain rods and lighting fixtures.

158. Perhaps the most unusual of Dixon's floor plans, this house features a living room set at forty-five degrees to the street, as well as a curving entry hall and an octagonal breakfast room. The portion of the second floor located behind the false-shuttered window was long left unfinished, perhaps due to a lack of resources brought on by the Great Depression. The oddly isolated stones set into the chimney depart from the more common Storybook practice of concentrating visually heavy materials in the lowest part of the elevation. The stone surrounding the entry arch, however, is a classic Storybook feature.

159. A dramatically curved hall opening onto a sunken living room are among the unique features of this, Dixon's most original home on Ross Street. The batten door visible at the right is typical of interior doors throughout the tract. The stone trim of the entryway arch can be glimpsed beyond the front door.

160. The sunken living room features an unusual coved ceiling with curving beams. The walls flanking the trademark Dixon fireplace are subtly curved outward, mirroring the room's opposite wall, which follows the curved entrance hall. The archway at the left opens to a foyer leading to the dining room, as well as onto a small walled patio. The pegged random-plank floor is typical of Revival-style homes of the 1920s.

162. The lamp-in-a-niche motif was a Dixon favorite, and it appears in foyers or on chimney breasts throughout the Ross Street tract.

163. Here is another of builder Ernest W. Urch's "Modest Mansions" on Ross Street. The miniature shuttered window beneath the corbeled projection once again shows architect Dixon employing small-scale elements to produce a deceptively manorial look. The projecting half-timbered dormer carried on corbels is also a bit of visual trickery—compare its size to that of the front door below.

161. *(Opposite)* Few bathrooms in Storybook Style homes have survived unmodified, but this one has been painstakingly preserved by the home's present and original owner. The 1920s represent the zenith of the ceramic-tile crafts during the twentieth century, and the degree of care lavished on this small bathroom is quite typical of the era. The bordered floor with its diagonal field tiles is a common design, as is the wainscot with its bullnose cap (the uppermost course of green tiles) and decorative "feature strip" just below it. Showers were customarily tiled on the interior, often including the ceiling, with door openings framed in tile as seen here.

164. This leaded-glass window with false shutters plays a trick of scale on the passerby—it measures a scant two feet in height. W. W. Dixon was the architect; Walter W. Urch the contractor.

165. *(Opposite)* Fine stonework on the entrance path, porch, and entrance arch distinguish this Dixon home on Ross Street. The projecting upper gable and small areas of half-timbering are vintage Dixon devices that appear on nearly every home in this tract. The chimney, with its attractively random rubble-stone trim, emulates the chimneys of French vernacular architecture.

CAMEOS

The United States in the early 1920s was blessed with an enormous range of skilled artisans—quite probably more than at any time before or since. Due to the burgeoning popularity of Period Revival styles during those years, the crafts of exterior plastering, blacksmithing, masonry, terra-cotta molding, and tilemaking were at their zenith. The Storybook Style, with its antiquarian aspirations and its penchant for the unusual, made full use of these consummate skills.

Much of the puckish nature of Storybook design resides in details that are not apparent until close viewing. Storybook architects and builders—more than any others of the twentieth century—paid great attention to features such as front doors, chimneys, and lighting fixtures.

The variations seen in Storybook entrance-door designs are almost limitless, yet they do exhibit recurring themes. Round-topped doors are quite popular, harking back as they do to the medieval masonry arch; however, such doors are generally seen on large homes due to their greater expense. Typical in both round-and square-topped versions are the various styles of "batten door," fashioned to resemble medieval plank doors bound together by horizontal rails or battens, and often braced by a decorative diagonal as well. Peek-a-boos, small viewing ports located in the body of the door, are also common. Frequently installed in the wall beside entrance doors are mail slots that receive letters in a small recessed chamber with a grillework door; with their modest capacity, they are reminders of a more genteel era not yet inundated by reams of junk mail.

Entrance doors also furnished a broad palette for the exceptional ironwork of the era. Hammered iron strap hinges in delicate plant-like forms are a favorite motif, as are rows of purely decorative, square-headed wrought nails. Wrought locksets provide another showcase for the blacksmith's art. Other ironwork—most having characteristically organic or serpentine motifs—can be found on stair and balcony railings, weathervanes, gates, and chimney braces.

Chimneys provided yet another outlet for Storybook whimsy. While some designs are recognizably derived from vernacular French, Spanish, or English prototypes, others are the singular creations of their designers. Square, rectangular, and circular ground plans are all common, and are often combined with either stepped or battered (or sloped) elevations. Chimney finishes were seldom limited to a single material; where the predominant finish was stucco, for example, the chimney might be set off by a pattern of brick quoins or a cast-stone relief panel, or feature random inclusions of rubble stone, brick, or both. Brick chimneys, on the other hand, might incorporate accents of rubble or ashlar in various quantities or locations. In Storybook tracts, developers quickly found that varying chimney designs was a cheap and effective way to distinguish homes built with identical floor plans.

Lighting fixtures are another area of astounding diversity; it is rare to see the same fixture recur in any two Storybook residences. In many cases, fixtures were borrowed from other home styles: the wrought-iron chandeliers often seen in Storybook dining rooms, for example, might have been originally intended for use in the concurrent Spanish Revival houses, while the popular hurricane-lamp pattern of sconce would have been quite at home in Colonial Revival designs of the era. Unlike their more popular contemporaries, Storybook Style homes were too scarce to warrant the commercial manufacture of their own "medieval" hardware lines, and it was common practice to install hardware items marketed for more popular styles as long as they suited the over-

166. A round-topped leaded-glass pane repeats the shape of the front door in Spokane's Randolph Smith house. The entrance is set in the base of a turret in classic Storybook fashion. Note also the stucco's exaggerated trowelmarks, another favorite technique for suggesting antiquity.

167. Underscaled lanterns and overscaled hinges give an intentionally cartoonish flavor to the entrance of this Long Beach home.

all Storybook feeling. In the absence of appropriate designs, or where budgets were unusually generous, fixtures were custom made to the architect's specifications.

It would be impossible to catalog the plethora of curious details employed by Storybook architects and builders. That is as it should be, for one of the style's greatest delights lies in the continual discovery of its eccentricities—the small surprises that have so happily transcended the passage of time, and still allow us a momentary glimpse into the spontaneous joy of their creation.

169. A delicate cast-iron gate and lunette are contrasted against bold quarry-faced ashlar in the entrance to this home in Washington, D.C.

168. *(Opposite)* Common brick, clinker brick, and stucco combine to produce an arrestingly textured entrance to this Santa Monica home (see fig. 47) dating from the late 1920s. The circular brick porch cleverly echoes the round-arched door, while the spiky lantern above it provides a counterpoint to the soft curving forms.

170. The lockset of this Carr Jones-designed home bears the unmistakable marks of hand forging. The popularity of the various European revival styles during the 1920s produced a national resurgence of demand for traditional handicrafts such as blacksmithing, wood carving, and tilesetting. Jones, an architect in the true medieval tradition of master builder, was well-versed in all of these crafts.

171. A doorknob escutcheon in the guise of a swordsman guards the entrance to this Seattle home.

172. A delicate scroll graces the superb entrance hardware on the door of this Walter W. Urch-built "Modest Mansion." Note the wave pattern of the door planking, which was originally varnished rather than painted. The architect was W. W. Dixon.

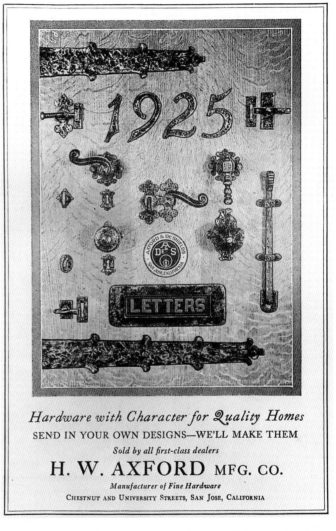

173. Like many other hardware manufacturers of the era, H. W. Axford of San Jose offered custom fabrication; this advertisement appeared in the February 1926 issue of W. W. Dixon's *The Home Designer and Garden Beautiful.*

174. In addition to being randomly studded with rubble stone, this cleverly designed chimney on Oakland's Ross Street boasts two patches of intentionally "'broken" stucco revealing the brick masonry beneath.

175. The randomly bricked corners and stucco field of this chimney are a common Storybook design feature inspired by various regional chimney styles seen in the vernacular buildings of the French countryside.

176. Unusually gawky proportions mark this otherwise familiar chimney design using brick studded with rubble stone.

177. Providing a broad canvas for the mason's craft, this massive chimney combines crazed brick and stone in a thoroughly eccentric form—serpentine on one side, stepped on the other, and terminating in an oddly diminutive flue.

178. Beehive chimneys are another frequent Storybook trait inspired by European vernacular chimney styles. This Mediterranean-derived example combines crazed-brick masonry and rubble stone, and is elegantly topped off by an arcaded cap and finial.

179. In this Oakland home crazed brickwork, leaded-glass casements, and a flower box slung on chains combine to transform a potentially dull expanse of wall into a visual and textural delight.

180. This unusual window grille in Asheville, North Carolina's Ellington House was flame-cut from a salvaged scrap of sheet steel; a pair of wood casements hide behind it.

181. A modern addition by the owner, this superb front gate with its naturalistic plant motif remains admirably true to the artistic spirit of Storybook design.

182. A graceful peak on the scrollwork of this unconventional wrought-iron railing defies the usual practice of using horizontal caprails. The bleached mahogany door beyond is ornamented with false studs imitating the hand-wrought fasteners of medieval times.

183. The living room of this Oakland home features a secret doorway straight out of a Hollywood thriller. What's behind it is a less-than-dramatic storage closet.

184. A pair of delicate
wrought-iron gates separates
the windowless dining room of
this Oakland home from an
adjoining glass-roofed foyer.

185. A massively and beautifully crafted wrought-iron pole lantern.

186. An unusual lamp with a pierced metal screen in lieu of the usual glass shade graces a Storybook cottage in San Francisco. The fixture was most likely custom made by a local manufacturer; note the especially clever means of concealing the electrical wiring within the hollow scroll bracket.

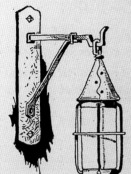
187. The Roberts Mfg. Co. of Oakland, which offered custom lighting fixtures "with a personality," was one of many such fixture suppliers of the era. Custom fabrication was common during the '20s, and it accounts for the surprising range of lighting fixture designs encountered in even modest homes.

188. The cap on this cast- and wrought-metal porch lamp recalls, perhaps not coincidentally, a World War I-era German spiked helmet.

189. Both of these delicate porch lamps combine cast iron and amber glass, one in a sconce style, the other surface-mounted.

190. What appears to be a rather Gothic-looking leaded-glass porch lamp on the outside of this Long Beach home is actually the rear of an interior niche lit by a fixture mimicking a candlestand. Also note the door for the interior mail chute visible in the exterior view. The house dates from 1928.

191. The 1920s was a time of great technical innovation in architecture, and homes of the era gave us built-in ironing boards, speaking tubes, convection-cooled fruit closets, built-in refrigeration, and even a radio loudspeaker built into a chandelier. The "Mailo-Box," which delivered mail to a home's interior via a chute concealed in the wall, was another of these forward-looking conveniences. It was widely advertised in *The Home Designer and Garden Beautiful,* and can be found in a large percentage of the era's houses.

192. A unique sconce in a stone-trimmed niche graces the foyer of this Dixon home on Oakland's Ross Street. A closer look reveals it to be nothing more than a standard ceiling fixture cleverly mounted upside-down.

193. A wrought-iron backing plate, scroll ornament, and scalloped lamp base make for a simple yet timeless sconce in this Santa Monica residence.

194. Spokane's Rosebush House is home to this spectacularly effusive sconce, whose deeply sculpted backing plate not only accommodates imaginary heraldry but also sprouts twin gargoyles that spew pendant fixtures from their mouths.

196. A delicately cast metal screen distinguishes this superb sconce in the dining room of Pasadena's Babcock residence.

195. Another Rosebush House fixture, this one has a more restrained but no less eclectic motif featuring a shield-shaped canopy, a scroll bracket, and a socket embellished with stylized leaves.

145

198. A wrought-iron ring forms the basis for this five-lamp pendant fixture in the dining room of a Santa Monica residence.

197. With its simple lines and delicate shell motif, this wall sconce in the foyer of the Babcock house shows a degree of Classical restraint seldom found in Storybook work.

199. A four-armed pendant fixture with the popular wrought-iron scroll motif hangs in the dining room of this home in Oakland's Ross Street tract.

147

200. A simple wrought-iron pendant lamp of the type frequently installed in foyers and halls. The sleeve with its dripping-wax effect is ubiquitous in Storybook construction.

201. A beautifully crafted, five-armed wrought-iron pendant fixture graces the dining room of a Piedmont, California, home.

ENCORES

Architectural fashions are inevitably cyclical, and it is only a matter of time before long-forgotten styles are rediscovered, celebrated, and finally reinterpreted in modern form. Yet some styles lend themselves to this process more readily than others. Colonial-era houses, for example, are remarkably well suited to modern reinterpretation, while Victorian-era houses are not. Likewise, while one might occasionally find a passable modern copy of a California Bungalow or a Spanish Revival cottage, recapturing the essence of a Storybook Style home has proved elusive to most who have attempted it. One reason for this is that the style relies heavily on spontaneity and whimsy—qualities that cannot be captured via today's necessarily slavish adherence to plans. Modern economics provides another reason: with labor currently comprising about two-thirds of the cost of a new home—a virtual reversal of 1920s conditions—the crafts-intensive, one-of-a-kind nature of Storybook Style designs demands a vast budget, unlimited sweat equity, or both.

Perhaps the nation's most startling modern-day interpretation of the Storybook Style is the residence of Richey and Karen Morgan, located in Olalla, Washington, just outside Tacoma. When asked what inspired them to begin this gigantic undertaking—now in its third decade and counting—the Morgans casually mention a brief visit they once made to the Fable Cottage in Vancouver, British Columbia, a little-known tourist attraction that is no longer extant. Yet one suspects that their real motivations lie closer to those of the original Storybook Style architects and builders: namely, a passion for craftsmanship, a love for the unique, and an optimism that manifests itself in the exuberant forms of this joyful style.

An earlier and equally fine example of modern Storybook design is the unique Los Angeles cottage built by a onetime Disney artist named Lawrence Joseph between 1946 and 1982. With its mushroom cap-like roof and its seemingly random design—in fact, the product of painstaking effort—the house is a fitting testament to both the artistry and craftsmanship of its builder. Known locally as the Egg House, it is a beloved neighborhood landmark, and has been designated a City of Los Angeles historic and cultural monument.

The Storybook Style is often referred to as being "Disneyesque," a term that is visually immediate but, except perhaps in the case of the Egg House and other late examples, one that is historically inaccurate. Walt Disney was born in Chicago in 1901, and arrived in Los Angeles in 1923. His first large-scale success in animated cartoons did not come until 1927, when he introduced a character known as Oswald the Lucky Rabbit. A year later, the ageless Mickey Mouse made his debut in a short cartoon called *Steamboat Willie.*

The sumptuous background art for which the Disney studio became justly renowned, and from which the adjective "Disneyesque" arises, did not appear until the early 1930s; it reached its apex in the studio's first feature-length animated film, *Snow White and the Seven Dwarfs*, released four days before Christmas in 1937. The fantastical buildings seen in these animated films often bear startling similarity to actual Storybook Style homes. By the time the films appeared, of course, the Storybook Style had already faded into history.

Perhaps it should come as no surprise that Walt Disney shared a background in The Great War along with many of the Storybook Style figures recounted earlier. In 1917, the sixteen-year-old Disney falsified his age and enlisted in the Navy, but the Armistice was signed before he saw action. He was nevertheless assigned to a military canteen in Neufchâteau, France—an experience that no doubt influenced him as much as it did practitioners of the Storybook Style. He returned to the United States in 1919 and founded a small cartoon studio in Kansas City, before making his historic move to Los Angeles four years later.

Whether we call them Disneyesque, Fairy Tale, Hansel and Gretel, or just plain home, the houses on these pages are proof of America's enduring fascination with the Storybook Style.

202. Certainly the country's
most spectacular modern-day
evocation of the Storybook
Style is Richey and Karen
Morgan's Olalla, Washington,
home, begun in 1980 and still
a work in progress. The
Morgans were inspired to
begin this undertaking after
touring a fanciful Storybook
cottage in Vancouver. As his
own contractor, Richey Morgan
has had to rediscover numerous
Storybook construction techniques, as well as invent a
number of new ones. He has
set down his hard-won experience in an informal guide to
Storybook design, complete
with sketches.

203. The Morgans handcrafted this three-hundred-pound front door using a chain saw, a belt sander, and a great deal of elbow grease. They also made the massive door knocker and the flame-cut hammered hinges.

204. The entrance path crosses a tiny brook and wends its way between clusters of boulders before reaching the front door. The paving is a modern version of the scored and colored steps frequently seen in Storybook construction.

205. Comically overscaled hinges decorate the massive handcrafted garage doors.

206. The other-worldly roofscape of the Morgan home viewed from the hillside behind it.

208. Superbly crafted masonry and woodwork make the Morgan home like no other. The valance and overhead beam were patiently carved with a chain saw and belt sander to bring out the natural forms of the wood.

209. A section of a cedar tree trunk five feet in diameter forms an archway between the kitchen and dining area. The staircase to the attic bedroom is just beyond.

207. *(Opposite)* Each of Morgan's unique doors is painstakingly handcrafted using a method of his own invention. Planks are roughly shaped using a chain saw and are then joined by horizontal rods passing through the width of the door. A small belt sander is used to mimic the texture of hand-adzing. Finally, the door is hung on flame-cut hinges—also made by Morgan—and the cement jamb is cast in place to fit it.

210. The attic bedroom, with its odd-shaped windows and its knobbly balustrade and ridge beam, is a true fairytale escape for children.

211. The medieval and the modern coexist in the Morgan kitchen, where a massive stone fireplace shares space with a built-in electric oven. The free-form openings suspended from the ceiling are constructed of plaster-covered wire mesh and contain storage space.

212. A fireplace of huge boulders and a naturalistic ceiling encrusted with stalactites stretch the Storybook genre into whole new realms.

213. Lawrence Joseph built this lovingly detailed cottage, known locally as the Egg House, between 1946 and 1982. Prior to World War II, Joseph had worked as an artist at the Walt Disney Studios, and the cottage's whimsical massing and absence of straight lines strongly suggest the comically misshapen structures seen in the backdrops of numerous Disney animated features.

214. Carmel-By-The-Sea, California, is the setting for this house designed in the spirit of local designer-builder Hugh Comstock, who in the late '20s almost single-handedly began Carmel's tradition of quaint architecture. The free-form half-timbering is especially reminiscent of Comstock's work, as is the patinated stucco finish.

215. Designer-builder Doug Allinger, the stepson of Carr Jones, has admirably upheld the tradition of his stepfather's designs in brick and timber. In his own work, such as this retail store in Walnut Creek, California, Allinger combines Jones's timeless palette of materials with his own gifted sense of composition to yield picturesque Storybook classics for a new generation.

216. Known as The Grove, these cottages by Los Angeles architect Allen Siple were built on the then-popular courtyard plan in 1932, with additions by Edla Muir in 1940. They were among the few surviving examples of Siple's courtyard designs when they were threatened by a major construction project in the 1980s. With popular support, the project's developers relocated the cottages to a nearby site in 1988 and reconfigured them for office use. Careful siting, exceptional attention to detail, and a superb landscaping scheme have succeeded in maintaining an authentic Storybook feel despite nearly total reconstruction.

217. No Storybook enclave is complete without at least one turreted home, and this one features a particularly robust example. The upstairs latticed "balcony" in the center foreground is a classic bit of Storybook visual trickery used to make this tiny cottage look much larger. To appreciate its miniature scale, compare it to the standard-size entrance doors below.

218. Clever tricks of scale are once again used to produce a quaint effect—compare the height of the left-side window to that of the normally scaled entrance door.

219. The "tree-trunk" posts of this rustic wishing well are a deception in the finest Hollywood tradition. They are actually made of wire-reinforced cement colored and sculpted to resemble bark.